next level SOUL™ PRESENTS

A Soul's Guide to
metaphysics and spirituality

A TRANSCENDENTAL JOURNEY

BY CONNIE H. DEUTSCH

Next Level Soul™ Presents: A Soul's Guide to Metaphysics and Spirituality: A Transcendental Journey

Copyright © 2022 by Connie H. Deutsch

All rights reserved. No portion of this publication may be reproduced stored in a retrieval system or transmitted by any means—electronic mechanical photocopying recording or any other—except for brief quotations in printed reviews without the prior written permission of the publisher.

Cover Art & Book Design: IFH Books
Photography by: Christopher Burns

Next Level Soul™ is a trademark of IFH Industries, Inc. All Rights Reserved.

IFH Books - A Division of IFH Industries Inc.
13492 N. Highway 183 #120-757
Austin, TX 78750
www.nextlevelsoul.com/books

Ordering Information:
Quantity sales: Special discounts are available on quantity purchases by corporations, associations and others. For details contact the publisher at the address above.

Orders by US trade bookstores and wholesalers:
Please contact the publisher at the address above.

Printed in the United States of America

ISBN Paperback: 979-8-9858940-2-8
First Edition

DEDICATION

We all have things that shaped our lives. For me, a few things stand out in vivid memory. In my day, girls weren't expected to go to college, and if they did go, there were snide remarks that they were only going to college to get their Mrs. Degree. In my house, that couldn't be further from the truth.

My parents were strong advocates of education. It was never a question of IF I went to college; it was always, WHEN I went to college and not graduating was not an option.

Achieving greatness was never expected of me but excellence was. One day, I was working on something and I couldn't get it to work. I was all set to give up and my mother said, "If at first you don't succeed, try, try, try again. And if you still don't succeed, keep trying until you do.

That set the stage for the rest of my life. To this day, I try to estimate what I think is possible for me to achieve because I know that I have to finish what I start, and it better be the best that I can do.

VIII • A SOUL'S GUIDE TO METAPHYSICS AND SPIRITUALITY

The thing that gave me the most pleasure growing up, and all the days of my life since then, was my relationship with my brothers. If everything was going topsy-turvy, a hug from one of them would lift my spirits. There was such goodness in them that it was like a beacon welcoming me home.

Michael took everything apart to see how it worked. Sometimes he put it back together again and sometimes he didn't. For him, the challenge was in seeing how it worked. Not too much has changed since those early years. He still loves learning and he still takes everything apart to see how it works but now he puts them back together when his curiosity is satisfied.

Kenny, the youngest, lined everything up in perfect order. If he was playing with miniature toy soldiers, they were arranged in perfect alignment. I have pictures of them at the Smithsonian, when they were young, and you can see by the expression on their faces that Michael was trying to figure out how things worked and Kenny was trying to figure out how to make sense out of what he was seeing.

They were the best part of my life. Kenny was taken from us a few years ago and we miss him so much. If I had to come up with an adjective to describe him, the word would be "noble." He was all that and more and he was loved by everyone.

I have always said that Michael is love incarnate. He has always been the epitome of love and goodness. No matter what life has handed him, you can still feel his unwavering love and goodness shining through.

My son, Bruce, gives me tremendous pleasure. I'm his greatest fan. When he embarks on something new, it doesn't occur to me that he might not be able to do it; I'm always so sure that he will succeed. And he always does, so my faith in him has never been misplaced. There is such innate goodness in him and he treats everyone respectfully so it is no surprise that he is liked and admired by everyone he meets.

I have been very blessed by having the love and support of my family all these years and, to them, I owe the greatest debt of gratitude for all they have given me and for all they have been.

TABLE OF CONTENTS

Introduction	1
Chapter 1: How Spiritual Are You?	4
Chapter 2: How to Perform Miracles	7
Chapter 3: The Spiritual Essence of Pond Scum	12
Chapter 4: Pet Lovers Wave Goodbye From Heaven	16
Chapter 5: I Was Left Behind	20
Chapter 6: Turning the Other Cheek	25
Chapter 7: Love and Fairy Dust	29
Chapter 8: Meditation Can be for Everyone!	33
Chapter 9: On the Way to Becoming	38
Chapter 10: Mirror, Mirror On the Wall	42
Chapter 11: Is it God's Will or Your Will?	46
Chapter 12: Thinking Outside the Box	50
Chapter 13: A Ghost Inside Him or A Past Life Memory?	54
Chapter 14: Waking up in Someone Else's Body	57
Chapter 15: Past Lives and Future Lives	60
Chapter 16: A Surreal Experience	63
Chapter 17: Nothing is Hopeless	66
Chapter 18: Do You Believe in Miracles?	69
Chapter 19: Is There a Reason for Everything?	72
Chapter 20: Beyond Belief	75

Chapter 21: My Life in a Fortune Cookie 78

Chapter 22: Morning Thoughts 81

Chapter 23: The Language of Tent Revivals 84

Chapter 24: Dreaming in Color 87

Chapter 25: Do You Believe in Affirmations? 90

Chapter 26: Pushing the Envelope 93

Chapter 27: A Woman Worth Knowing 96

Chapter 28: There's No Such Thing as ESP? 99

Chapter 29: That Old Time Religion 102

Chapter 30: I'm Only Human 105

Chapter 31: Our Changing Values 110

Chapter 32: Deaf Composer a Fraud 114

Chapter 33: Modern Day David and Goliath 117

Chapter 34: Elderly First-Time Mothers 120

Chapter 35: Two Sides to the Story 123

Chapter 36: Exposed: Groom-To-Be Faked His Own Death 126

Chapter 37: The Height of Idiocy 129

Chapter 38: Hold Onto Your Wallet 132

Chapter 39: Fired? Laid Off? Get a Virtual Résumé 135

Chapter 40: Deathbed Promises 138

Chapter 41: A Good Liar 141

Chapter 42: Posting a Bad Review? Think Again 144

Chapter 43: The Judge Does Stand-up Comedy 147

Chapter 44: Banana Peel Lawsuit Leads to Arrest 150

Chapter 45: Cherished Memories   153

Chapter 46: Living in a Disposable World   156

Chapter 47: Choosing Your Battles Carefully   159

Chapter 48: After Your Gift Has Been Delivered   163

Chapter 49: Is It Really Better to Give Than to Receive? 167

Chapter 50: Why Don't People Grieve Alike?   170

Chapter 51: Why Do People Disappoint Us?   173

Chapter 52: Instant Trust, Instant Betrayal   176

Chapter 53: Having it All   179

Chapter 54: What Fairy Tales Taught Us   182

Chapter 55: Is it Kindness or Cowardice?   185

Chapter 56: My Spiritual Playground   188

Chapter 57: My Spiritual Toy Box   199

Chapter 58: The Age of Enlightenment   216

Chapter 59: Superman's Kryptonite   222

Chapter 60: In My Opinion . . .   226

About the Author   232

What is Next Level Soul?   233

Thoughts and Reflections   235

INTRODUCTION

When I was very young, I used to question how do we know that there is a god if we can't see Him? My father's answers never satisfied me. He would say things like, "We can identify the presence of a rose by its smell even if we cannot see it; the same with the presence of God. We may not be able to see Him but if we're still and listen intently, we can feel His presence."

Several years later, as a college freshman, I was put in a philosophy course for seniors. No one realized the mistake until the middle of the semester when it was too late to correct their error.

My first week in this senior philosophy class was a nightmare. To this day, I never did figure out "when is a table not a table?" We studied all the great philosophers and not once did I come across the answer to when is a table not a table? After I graduated, I looked in the Classified Ads for a job as a philosopher and to my great disappointment, there were no job listings for that kind of work.

The odd thing about this was that from the time I was very young to the present day, I have always been intrigued by the subjects of metaphysics and spirituality. I emphasize spirituality and not religious. There are many spiritual people who are atheists and many very religious people who are not the least bit spiritual. Hence, the differentiation between the two.

Unfortunately, many people think that being spiritual means being saintly and nothing could be further from the truth. Being spiritual is another way of saying be kind and loving and refrain from being judgmental.

We all make mistakes and a spiritual person, when realizing he has inadvertently hurt someone, will try to make amends. We all have good days and bad days so it is possible that on the good days we try to be the best we can possibly be. Believe it or not, this is really a choice. We can choose to be loving and kind or we can choose to exhibit a mean streak. The choice is ours.

If we want to accrue positive karma, we can think of it as a spiritual bank account. Every time you do something for the good of mankind, you raise the vibration of the universe and you deposit positive karma into your spiritual bank account. If you are unkind to someone, all of mankind feels the negative vibration and this lowers the vibration of the universe, thereby decreasing the amount of positive karma in your spiritual bank account.

I think the easiest way to remember the laws of the universe is to ask yourself if you would like to be the one who is receiving the treatment you are doling out. If the answer is no, find another way of addressing the current problem. But keep in mind that your every thought, action, and emotion are recorded in the Akashic Records for all eternity and are being added to your spiritual bank account.

- Connie H. Deutsch

CHAPTER 1
HOW SPIRITUAL ARE YOU?

One of the most valuable lessons I learned in my quest for higher consciousness is that spiritual is, as spiritual does. It's one thing to sit in an ashram meditating and chanting Aum, and have deep philosophical discussions with other like-minded people about how the soul is to the body as the spirit is to God, and it's another thing to make these discussions an embodiment of your life.

I once taught a class called "Practical Mysticism in Today's Busy Society" and the basis for that class was to take the spiritual concepts that we read about and talk about, and bring them into our daily lives.

One of the stories I shared with them was about a disciple who said to his guru, "I am very anxious to attain God-consciousness. How can I be more spiritual?" His guru asked him if he had eaten breakfast. The disciple said that he had and his guru asked him if he washed his dishes when he had finished.

He told his disciple that responsibility and caring for others is the way to enlightenment. When you expect others to shoulder your responsibilities and you don't have enough love in your heart to try to lighten their load, you miss the opportunity to advance your soul.

Many people don't realize that every relationship gives us another chance to "grow" our soul. The parent who puts the safety and well-being of his child before his own desires is far more spiritual than the person who prays and meditates every day but who is indifferent to the plight of others.

Someone who takes care of a terminally ill friend or relative, who gives of himself without thought of recompense, is living a spiritual life; he doesn't need books or seminars to tell him how to be spiritual; he already is.

When we see people volunteering their time to take care of those less fortunate, we see spirituality in living action. These people don't need lessons; they are already incorporating the laws of the universe into their daily lives.

The measure of one's spirituality lies in the depth of his love and in the care he gives to the important people in his life; it can also be seen in the way he treats the rest of humanity when he has nothing to gain and when he thinks no one is watching.

Natural disasters and national emergencies tend to bring us closer together and remind us that we share a common bond; it puts things into perspective when we realize how much we need one another to survive these tumultuous events. When we come to the aid of those whose lives would be more difficult without our help, this is spirituality in its finest hour.

So what is spirituality and why does it seem so elusive? It is simply the principle of treating others as you wish to be treated and not deliberately causing anyone harm.

Although it is very hard to live in this consciousness twenty-four hours a day, the concept is very simple. For most of us, we have moments of great spirituality and moments of temporal reminders that we have a long way to go before we reach self-mastery. And through it all, we keep longing for that oneness with God and trying anything and everything to attain it.

CHAPTER 2
HOW TO PERFORM MIRACLES

We might not be able to part the Red Sea or turn water into wine but each of us has the ability to perform smaller miracles. For those who don't have the ability to focus well enough, or who are too impatient to work at it long enough, if the desire and determination are present and you practice one of the smaller miracles, you can at least get the reaction from people, "Oh, WOW!! How did you do that?"

We start with the premise that thought, cloaked in desire, becomes a reality and that what the mind conceives, you can achieve. What this boils down to is that first you have to want something so badly that you can almost taste it. You have to eat it, sleep it, breathe it until it becomes your reality.

At this point, I should mention that you better be careful about wanting something so much because at some point, you will get it. There is an old saying that I'm sure each of us has grown up with, "Be careful what you wish for because you might get it."

Miracles are performed by moving atoms and molecules to bring matter into being. By rearranging those atoms and molecules you can stop something from manifesting or make it manifest. It takes a lot of energy and intense concentration but each of us has the power to create miracles with visualization.

Paramahansa Yogananda, an Indian yogi, wrote about the law of miracles in his book, *Autobiography of a Yogi*. He said, "The actual form of the projection (whatever it be: a tree, a medicine, a human body) is determined by the yogi's wish and by his power of will and of visualization."

When I first got into metaphysics, I read everything I could get my hands on. I was so intrigued with the various concepts I was learning about that I tried my hand at doing everything from stopping a torrential downpour long enough for me to get in and out of my car and go into and out of stores, to telling the universe that I had bills to pay and I needed x amount of money by a certain date, to raising people's vibrations without them being aware that I was moving atoms and molecules to accomplish it.

It was such an exciting time. During those early years, nearly four decades ago, there had been so much written about the art of visualization that it was a no-brainer that my curiosity would lead me to experiment with it. Every day, I would spend several hours training my mind to visualize something that I wanted to occur and I would wait in eager anticipation for it to happen.

I soon realized that there were a few key elements that had to be included, in addition to having a strong desire to make it happen or stop it from happening. I also had to see it in my mind's eye, in its entirety, and know with every fiber of my being that it would materialize exactly as I had seen it.

I was having so much fun performing these minor miracles with just my mind, that I visualized everything I could think of just for the sheer pleasure of being able to accomplish the most challenging tasks.

One day I received a gorgeous floral arrangement as a gift. It was in a beautiful delft blue ceramic pot and it looked and smelled heavenly. I loved it. While most people have a green thumb, I have always had a black thumb. As much as I love flowers and plants, they usually die under my care.

After a few days, some of the flowers in this arrangement looked a bit wilted. I truly wanted to preserve them so I tried to visualize them being restored to their former health.

Every day I would water the flowers and put my hands around them, visualizing healing rays going into them. Then I would remove the dead flowers and continue to visualize the remaining ones getting healthier.

I had told my friend about the experiment I was doing and we arranged to speak to each other once a day to track my progress.

Every day I would call her to tell her that the experiment was working on the cut flowers because some of them still looked beautiful and fresh. About two weeks later, I accidentally touched one of the bottom flowers and discovered that the reason they still looked so beautiful and fresh was because they were artificial.

While visualization might not work on healing artificial flowers, at least for those who have not yet reached yogi status, it does work on a multitude of other things.

For those who are eager to learn how to perform miracles, start with something easy, something that is within the realm of possibility, and have it be something you truly desire. Visualize it until you see it so clearly in your mind's eye that you can almost feel the atoms and molecules being rearranged to make your wish come true. Then put the full force of your will behind it and expect it to happen and it will happen.

CHAPTER 3
THE SPIRITUAL ESSENCE OF POND SCUM

I have always liked experimenting with concepts and one of the concepts I experimented with was the sending of divine love and light to the spirit of God within a person.

I wanted to see if I could change a person's attitude and make him into a more loving being after a lifetime of abusing others. I discovered that while it is not an easy task, it is more than possible to accomplish. It just takes perseverance and a desire to raise the vibration of someone for the higher good of that person.

During those early years, when everything was fresh and new, and all the years afterward, I have sent divine love and light to the spirit of God within many people. In the beginning, when I ran up against someone who was being exceptionally difficult, I would force myself to remember that while his personality may be that of pond scum, his spirit was that of God, and I would continue to send divine love and light to the God within him.

In the beginning, this was a very difficult concept for me to embrace because I didn't want to be a hypocrite. I kept imagining that the personality and the spirit within were one and the same.

Since I was looking at this concept with my emotions rather than my head, it didn't make sense to me that someone who was being obnoxious could also contain the essence of God within himself. In my mind, someone who was capable of deliberately causing others deep pain couldn't possibly have a spiritual essence.

I had to prove to myself that this separation of personality and spirit was very real and that if I overlooked the personality, I could actually feel the power of God's love pouring through me as I was sending it to someone else.

That feeling was so awesome that I started using that theory in the classes I was teaching. I gave my students a homework assignment. They were to pick one person with whom they felt an animosity and every day, for the remainder of our classes, they were to send divine love and light to that person. Then they had to report back to us and tell us the results.

While the homework assignment was highly successful with my students, it was not quite so successful with one of my clients. She told me that for years after hearing me talk about the divine spark, she would visualize this tiny spark, this little candle, being in the center of someone she didn't like, and she would send the prayer to that little spark. However, when she finally realized that this spark was larger than life, she said to me, "Now that I know we're not talking about a teensy little spark, I don't know if I can keep sending divine love and light to people I don't like."

My objective in those classes was to expose my students to different theories, not to convince them that any of these theories was absolute. I'm a firm believer that the only way we can fully believe something is if we experience it for ourselves.

I don't know if my client ever did have the experience but at least she had a theory that might rumble around in her head until life presented her with an opportunity to try it. If she didn't, then she will have to live with having people in her life whose vibrations are unpleasant. If she did have the experience then she has discovered one of the many keys to happiness.

CHAPTER 4
PET LOVERS WAVE GOODBYE FROM HEAVEN

When I first heard the story, I thought it was hilarious. It consists of two different versions: one version is that, according to prophesy, the end of the world will happen on May 21, 2011 and the other version does not give a date for the end of the world but says it's coming and they both address the concept of Rapture.

The simplified definition of Rapture is that God will be taking all those who believe in Him up to heaven just at the moment that He pulls the plug on Earth and causes our planet to cease to exist.

Apparently, there is a website that tells God-loving pet lovers that while they will be Raptured, their pets will not be because they have no soul. Therefore, this man, a self-proclaimed atheist, says that for a fee of $110.00 a pet, and $15.00 for each additional pet, he and his team of people who are too bad to be Raptured, will take care of these dogs and cats and provide a good home for them. There is a ten-year contract that the owners sign giving permission to have their pets taken after they have been Raptured.

The poor rabbits, horses, goats, chickens, ducks, and other assorted animals/pets, are not included in this contracted pet care after their owners have been Raptured. What happens to them? And how does he know that animals don't have a soul? He might have said that he received a message from God that animals don't have a soul, but since he says that he's an atheist, he can't use that story.

I'm not questioning religious people's right to believe in the Rapture theory; what I am questioning is that there isn't a whole lot of critical thinking taking place before they fork over $110.00 for the peace of mind of knowing that their pet will be looked after when they are no longer around to do so.

What I can't get my head around is that in none of the versions that I've heard, if this is truly the end of the world and the only people who are going to be saved are those who believe in God, where are these godless people going to be living with their countless dogs and cats?

I also can't imagine anyone handing someone they have never met or heard of, a fee of $110.00 to take care of their pet after they are gone. A guy hands them a contract that says he'll take care of their pet but they are to have no contact with him while they are still here on earth and he doesn't even want to meet their precious Fido or Kitty before he comes calling for them at the time of their Rapture. He doesn't even tell them where he is going to house all these animals or if there are zoning laws that allow him to keep so many of them on his property, if, indeed, he even has a property.

There are a few different stories about the details. In one story, this enterprising man has twenty-six godless rescuers in twenty-two states who have signed an affidavit that says they don't believe in God but they are animal lovers. In another story, these rescuers haven't signed an affidavit saying they don't believe in God but they are too bad to get into heaven yet they have passed a criminal background check. In yet another version, these rescuers are evil, but they are pet-loving people who can't get into heaven but they haven't had a criminal background check.

All the stories seem to be saying the same thing about the popularity of this website and the fact that this man has been making a lot of money playing on the emotions of people who want peace of mind at any price. Since this is a nonrefundable fee of $110.00, I wonder what the policy is if their precious pet dies before they get Raptured or what happens to their pet if they should die before the end of the world and before their Rapture.

What I'm not wondering about is the fact that this man has hit on a brilliant scheme to earn a living without having to invest a penny, without having to curry favor with an impossible employer, and without having to employ workers and be required to provide health insurance for them.

He can also laugh all the way to the bank knowing that he can continue to live as he's always lived, albeit a lot wealthier, giving peace of mind to people who believe in what he is offering, and feeling that he has caused no real damage.

CHAPTER 5
I WAS LEFT BEHIND

May 21, 2011, 5:55 PM, I looked at my clocks and synchronized them in preparation for the Rapture. At 6:05 PM, I looked at my synchronized clocks and decided that the Rapture must have come and gone, leaving me behind, because I was still here.

This got me to thinking about the spiritual meaning of the Rapture. Many decades ago, I had read about the theory that when Judgment Day came, there were going to be 144,000 spiritual people who were going to be admitted to heaven, leaving everyone else behind. I wondered about that. The theory didn't stipulate that the 144,000 people had to be religious or that they had to believe in God, only that they had to be spiritual.

Spiritual vs. Religious. Spirituality vs. Religiosity. And that was how I became interested in metaphysics and Universal Laws.

I started wondering what heaven would look like with untold numbers of religions and sects vying for first place at the right hand of God. Would it resemble a traffic jam with bumper-to-bumper Baptists, Catholics, Protestants, Jews, Buddhists, Methodists, Muslims, and numerous other religions from around the world in a holding pattern, each proclaiming that their way is the only way and wondering why nonbelievers were not in hell, or at least the nonbelievers of their particular religion were not in hell?

And then I started thinking that 144,000 spiritual people from all over the world isn't very many at all. That would be a very sad commentary on our civilization and not a very optimistic one, at that.

Just 144,000 spiritual people out of billions of people on the planet? If it was 144,000 spiritual people in your state or in your country, I could imagine people looking at each other and wondering if they were more spiritual than their neighbor.

But in the whole world? People would have no real standard of measurement to ascertain who their competition was. But then, again, that, in itself would be very unspiritual.

Spiritual is as spiritual does. Our spiritual selves are not in competition with others but within ourselves, to prod us to live in accordance with the higher laws of the universe rather than the man-made laws.

It is the innate drive within each of us to live in accordance with the spirit of the law rather than the letter of the law. And whether we recognize this force within us on a daily basis, it is there nonetheless and, in moments of clarity, we acknowledge our actions in the larger scheme of things.

So, that brings us back to my musings about Judgment Day and why I figured I was left behind when the Rapture came. I thought about my life and what I had contributed to humanity. I also thought about what I had accomplished and what I had failed to accomplish. This left quite a checklist.

Since I'm female, and born in an era when women were supposed to be the heart of the home, nurturer, caretaker, and living in a man's world, I figured I was a dismal failure. In my day, women were supposed to be good cooks and seamstresses, or at least know how to sew a button on a garment; that eliminated me as a candidate for experiencing the Rapture.

I once remarked to someone that I wasn't the domestic goddess of my county, to which the response was, "You're not the domestic goddess of the planet."

I have always believed that if we're still here on earth, then we haven't accomplished our mission and we still have much more work to do. If God is keeping a score card on each of us, and if one of the things I was supposed to learn in this life is how to love cooking and cleaning and letting others solve my problems so that I wouldn't have to worry "my pretty little head," then I figure I'll still be left behind when the real Armageddon comes around.

There has been so much hoopla over the Rapture and all the people who were preparing for it in sundry ways and having to live with the disappointment of not being able to leave their earthly responsibilities behind, that it makes me wonder if God would really let us know the time and date of Judgment Day. I think not.

Apparently, Apple shares that belief because I heard that they came out with a new app called iRapture and one of their employees said that it was hoped that the Rapture would really come on May 21st because then they wouldn't have to attend a boring meeting on May 22nd.

CHAPTER 6
DOES TURNING THE OTHER CHEEK MAKE YOU A VICTIM?

The essence of spirituality, also known as the universal karmic eraser or the state of grace, is love and forgiveness, of others and of ourselves. This does not mean that you have to accept inappropriate behavior from others, nor should you; to do so would signify that you don't love and respect yourself.

We are told to turn the other cheek. If you take this literally, then you would allow someone to keep abusing you, sometimes with an apology and a promise afterwards to never do it again, sometimes not. If you apply those words literally, you would become a victim, always turning the other cheek and forgiving the offender. But when you look at that statement from a universal perspective, you see it quite differently.

Think of what it means for a human to be made in God's image. This does not mean that man has the physical attributes of God or the personality of God, but that he has the divine spark within, or the spirit of God within him. In other words, he has the seed of perfection within him. Now, when we say to turn the other cheek, we can understand that the larger definition is to honor the God within, the spirit, while dealing differently with the personality of the soul.

When I first learned about this difference, I tried to get used to separating the personality from the spirit of someone who had always treated me badly. She had a cruel streak and we never liked each other, but we were always thrown into each other's company. I decided to try an experiment to see if I couldn't diffuse the antipathy between us and direct my prayers to the God within her, bypassing her personality.

At night I would pray, "Please God, send your love and light to the divine spark within her," and here I would grit my teeth and, practically snarling, say, "because God knows she *needs* it."

After a few months of doing this, I was told that she was going to be at the same home where I was invited. Before I left my house, I visualized the white light of protection going around me, shielding me from negativity. Then I visualized divine light preceding me and filling up the house that I was driving to. Then I visualized this woman being surrounded by God's love and light. I made sure to see it as *God's* love, not mine, because I knew I didn't love her, and I didn't want to feel like a hypocrite.

When I got to the house, I again put the white light of protection around myself . . . "You can never have enough of God's protection," I assured myself, and then I went inside. I looked around for this woman and when I saw her I made myself acknowledge her. She mumbled a greeting but didn't look at me. I thought to myself that this was indeed a major change. Instead of being my adversary, she was withdrawing. Well, that simply would not do. Not after all those months of sending her divine love.

During the rest of the evening I kept addressing questions to her that she had to answer because everyone expected her to; I made sure to ask her about things that required more than a monosyllabic answer. At no time did she look me in the eye; this was a first. I took encouragement from that.

In the months that followed, I continued to send her God's love and light in my daily prayers. Eventually, she started to respond. I was relentless. I increased the frequency and intensity of my prayers always sending God's love and light to the Divine spark within her. I also stopped gritting my teeth and adding the tag line, "because God knows she *needs* it."

In time, I became a favorite of hers and she started calling me on the telephone. I didn't want to become her favorite; I just wanted her to stop her animosity. I achieved more than my goal. It also showed me the power of sending divine love and light to the God within a person and to be able to witness how transformative it could be.

CHAPTER 7
LOVE AND FAIRY DUST

For the first several years after I got into metaphysics, it was such a heady feeling to hear myself being referred to as a "lightworker," one who is here to bring love and light to the world, to teach, by example, the higher principles of the universe, and to help heal the planet. I inwardly chuckled at the mental image I had of me gaily skipping all around the world, bringing this love and light to everyone.

I could see myself sprinkling it like one would sprinkle fairy dust, over those who needed it. It took me several years to realize that not only do lightworkers have to stand in line at the checkout counter of supermarkets, argue over errors in their bills, wait for repairmen to show up to fix their broken appliances, and get stuck in rush hour traffic, but that anyone who treats people lovingly, with kindness and respect, is considered a lightworker.

This shouldn't be confused with being saintly every minute of every day of our life, although that would be a refreshing change, but in most circumstances, we should take care that we don't do anything to actively cause people to suffer. We can't prevent the sufferings of mankind but we can at least do our part not to contribute to it.

If ever we needed lightworkers, the time is now. There is so much violence in the world that parents are afraid to let their children play in front of the house for fear of drive-by shootings and gang wars. It's an illusion to think that any of us are safe. You used to be worried about being mugged when you were walking home in the dark. Now you're worried about being mugged in the light of day.

Where are the lightworkers when we need them? Mother Teresa personified the ideal of a lightworker but she is gone. Martin Luther King and Mahatma Gandhi were our inspiration but they, too, are gone. The world needs more of these special people to light the way for the rest of us. And yet, from time to time, I still see people who are not famous light the way for us.

Every so often we will see a teacher or a nurse, a doctor or a musician, an artist or a construction worker light the way for us by living the principles of spirituality on a daily basis. They don't need religious leaders or do-gooders telling them how to be spiritual; they just are spiritual.

There was a story about a group of missionaries who wanted to bring the word of God to a primitive tribe. They spent several weeks with these people indoctrinating them into the teachings of the masters. When it was time for them to leave, they said goodbye to their new students and left in their boat. A little while later they looked back in shock to see these unworldly people running across the water trying to catch up with them and yelling that they forgot something that the missionaries had taught them. They didn't need to be taught to be spiritual; they were the living embodiment of spirituality.

We make such a mystery of the term, "spiritual" and it really is so easy. That is to say that the *concept* is easy, but living it can be an upward struggle, especially when your teenaged child tells you that he borrowed your new car and drove it into a fence, causing just enough damage to run up a large bill at the body shop but not enough damage for the insurance company to declare it "totaled."

CHAPTER 8

MEDITATION CAN BE FOR EVERYONE!

There are probably as many ways to get into a meditative state as there are leaves on a tamarind tree. There are also almost as many theories about when, where, and how a person should meditate. Although the classical teachers of meditation would unarguably classify this as heresy, I think that for each of us, it probably comes down to a personal preference.

How often have you heard different variations of the same theme: that if you want to reach the plane of God-consciousness, you have to meditate at 3:00 A.M. or when the fingers of dawn stretch across the sky?

It makes one question whether the experts can possibly mean that the people who work the night shift and don't get home until nine or ten o'clock in the morning are not spiritual and are doomed to never being able to be at One with God. There are many who would have you believe that this is so, or they would find day jobs.

Meditation is a very personal thing for most people. Some prefer to follow the breath while others choose to chant Aum and merge with the sound. Still, there are others who get into meditation more easily by clearing their head of all thoughts and entering that quiet space where they can feel God's presence.

They may use a technique of visualizing a simple object, like a plain teaspoon, keeping it firmly in their mind's eye, seeing nothing else and thinking nothing else, until they merge with that God presence.

It is essential to remember that because we are in human form, we have our good days and our bad days, and on our good days, our meditation will transcend us to the ultimate level, and on our bad days, we will be too preoccupied or too fidgety to get into a deep meditation.

On the days when your mind is too distracted to meditate effectively, get up and do something else for awhile. Then try again. Give yourself three attempts. If, on the third attempt, you are still struggling to quiet your mind, tell yourself that tomorrow is another day and give yourself permission to call it quits for today.

We often hear that spiritual people have to meditate at certain hours or that meditation can only be done a certain way, but that's not true. There are many people who meditate at the prescribed times and who do moonlight meditations and special holiday meditations, but who don't live spiritual lives.

As long as you are meditating for yourself and not for an audience, it doesn't matter when you meditate or where you meditate, the results will be the same: a communion with the God within. I truly doubt if God cares whether you meditate at three in the morning or at nine in the evening, as long as your motivation is to seek Him out.

There is another aspect of meditation that is too often overlooked, and that is the one of using meditation for relaxation or to change sleeping patterns, or to get an extra surge of energy. Insomniacs have been known to get a good night's sleep by meditating right before going to bed. They have also found that if they get tired during the day, a quickie meditation of fifteen or twenty minutes, will restore their energy for another six or eight hours.

During moments of stress when nothing is going right, you can change your vibration with a fifteen- or twenty-minute meditation, and that will change the outcome of your day. But be aware, that if three negative things happen to you within the same day, it is probably not the fault of other people; more likely, the fault is within you. That's when you should stop whatever you are doing and take time out to meditate for fifteen or twenty minutes. It will change how you affect other people and their reactions to you.

I think meditation can be for everyone. It affects your health, your mind, your attitude, your interpersonal relationships, your productivity, and your life.

Don't worry about whether it will make you spiritual; if you are living according to the precepts of the Golden Rule: Do unto others as you would have others do unto you and also the converse: Do not do to others what you do not want others to do to you, then meditation will help you attain God-consciousness. If you are not living that kind of life, then all the meditation, all the books, lectures, and seminars in the world will not move you to that level.

Meditation should be seen as a reward, not a discipline or a chore. It is a time of healing the human spirit and infusing a person with courage to get through the day; it is also the balancing of energies within the body, bringing mind, body, and spirit into perfect alignment, and it should not be confused with prayer. Prayer is when you speak to God; meditation is when you are still enough to hear God speak to you. If you haven't yet experienced the joys of meditating, start now.

Find your own rhythm, choose a time of day or night that works for you and don't be afraid to vary it. Use it to propel you to another level of spirituality or use it to help you sleep, to change your vibration, or to give you a quick spurt of energy, but use it. Rejoice in the myriad ways of bringing meditation into your life.

CHAPTER 9
ON THE WAY TO BECOMING

From the time we are born, we are always on our way to becoming something. We are embryos on our way to becoming a child. We are children on our way to becoming teenagers who think we know everything. We are teenagers who are as smart as we will ever be, on our way to becoming adults. We are adults who are as informed as we will ever be, on our way to becoming elderly. We are old now and we have a whole journey to look back on and see how far we have come, on our way to becoming.

Our journey through life is made up of myriad parts, some wonderful, some not so wonderful, some good, some bad, but all of them contribute their essential learning experiences to what we have become.

They say, "That which does not kill us makes us stronger." I don't subscribe to that theory. It implies that we have thought about the things that haven't killed us, but we have only to look around, talk to people, listen to their stories and get their points of view, to know that many of them have survived without becoming stronger. Many of them have survived without learning a single thing or being any wiser. They have simply survived and endured.

I was talking to a man who had survived a severe stroke. The doctors didn't expect him to live beyond that night. His wife and several of her friends gathered around his hospital bed and prayed over him all night. He survived. He couldn't talk or move parts of his body or communicate in any intelligible way and the doctors told his wife that he was going to be brain damaged, a vegetable. She would not accept that.

Once again, she marshaled her forces and she and her friends prayed over him, day and night, alternating shifts so that, for the next few months, he was never alone and never without a few of them praying over him.

A few years later, they came to visit me. He was walking perfectly, speaking perfectly, and using his fine mind the way he always had. When they told me what he had endured, I asked him if he had changed any part of his life as a result of that experience. He seemed surprised by the question and said, "No, when I recovered I went back to business as usual. Nothing has changed. Was it supposed to?"

In my thinking, when one survives a life-defining moment, everything changes. Your perception about life and death takes on new meaning. Your perception about disability and your resulting limitations has to change. Your understanding of important issues becomes sharper, more acute. Your relationships have to undergo subtle changes, and he said he didn't experience any of the things I put before him.

How does one undergo a near-death encounter and not change a single thing in one's thinking or in one's actions? And yet, he and his wife both agreed that not a single thing had changed.

What happened on his way to becoming? Did he miss some steps along the way? Did he not question his mortality or the meaning of life? Did he not experience a deeper connection to God for having his mind and body restored to 100% health? He claims not.

So, apparently you can survive near-death experiences, be restored to perfect health after losing bodily and mental functions and not become stronger physically, mentally, or emotionally. You can go through soul-destroying moments without becoming wiser or more spiritual. You can even escape the journey of being on the way to becoming. You can just become older without being on the way to becoming anything else.

CHAPTER 10
MIRROR, MIRROR ON THE WALL

When I first became interested in metaphysics, it was very discouraging to pick up book after book and read about all the psychics who appeared to have cornered the market on spirituality. They wrote prolifically about meditation, yoga, and God, although not necessarily in that order.

There were numerous "how-to" books on the subject of self-actualization and the discipline required to attain that exalted state. It seemed as if, like Athena, springing full-grown from the head of Zeus, all these psychics were born in a state of grace, fully perfected, with none of the flaws that the rest of us mere mortals possessed. They seemed to have never had an unspiritual thought, word, or deed, or experienced mundane problems like the rest of us.

Eventually, I realized that psychic does not equate with spiritual and that there are a lot of "phony holies" out there writing and teaching about the road to God-consciousness.

These "phony holies" were in competition with each other trying to be perceived as the most godlike. It was almost as if everyone was gazing into the magic mirror and asking, "Mirror, mirror on the wall, who is the most spiritual one of all?"

It was a wonderful learning experience. It taught me that a person can be very psychic without being the least bit spiritual and that a spiritual person, though usually very psychic, may not even be aware of it.

People are often more enchanted with psychic gifts than attaining God-consciousness. And in a way I can't blame them. Psychic ability can be trained and within a relatively short period of time they can see proof of this phenomenon.

They can practice sending and receiving messages through the ethers just by thinking and visualizing. They can send healing to people and plants and see quick results. They can see auras and hear voices. They can perform all their parlor tricks and look mighty impressive.

On the other hand, no one can actually see God-consciousness. I'm not even sure they can feel it when they are in the presence of someone who has reached that level.

So, why would the masses prefer to go through the long, arduous journey of self-realization when they can slide through life just using God's gifts?

If they were more concerned about their spiritual selves everyone would be acting more humanely to each other. Violence wouldn't keep exacerbating in every corner of the world.

There wouldn't be a culture of people who have entitlement issues. We wouldn't be surrounded by greed, hatred, and bigotry. We would be searching for the God within and sending God's love and light to everyone in the universe.

But that isn't happening. We complicate our search for God-consciousness by focusing on the psychic potential, which is the by-product of spirituality, instead of on God which is its essence.

It brings to mind the story of the man who is reunited with his guru after many years. The guru asks, "How have you spent these last twenty years, my son?" and his disciple says, "I have been learning how to walk on water." The guru shakes his head sadly and says, "What a waste of time and spiritual energy. Why didn't you just take a boat?"

Between now and the end of our life we need to ask ourselves if we have wasted our spiritual energy by settling for the illusion of spirituality by walking on water instead of taking a boat and striving to become one with God.

CHAPTER 11
IS IT GOD'S WILL OR YOUR WILL?

When your wishes remain unfulfilled and your life feels like one long, unremitting, struggle to overcome an endless array of obstacles, can you tell the difference between God's will and your will?

More often than I care to recall, I have heard people throw up their hands in defeat and declare, "It's God's will that this has happened" or "It's God's will that this hasn't happened." It doesn't occur to them that God doesn't take away a person's free will, nor does He stop them from trying other avenues to make something work to His advantage.

If you study the lives of successful people, you will see a golden thread of truth, that the people who overcome adversity and attain their dreams, are the people who don't give up; they are the ones who keep trying until they succeed. In the midst of their ordeal, they realize they may have to approach the situation with the mindset of Winston Churchill who said, "The pessimist sees difficulty in every opportunity. The optimist sees the opportunity in every difficulty."

It's no secret that people don't like to change. They may love new things, love new adventures, love meeting new people, but they don't love to change anything about themselves. It's so much easier to say that it's Gods will than to take responsibility for the way they live their lives.

I knew someone who had been diagnosed with Parkinson's Disease. He had gone the route of allopathic medicine and the disease was making huge inroads on his body. He wouldn't countenance changing his diet, doing things to relieve his stress levels, resting when he was tired, dressing in clothing that he didn't have to wrestle on and off his body, or looking into alternative health modalities that wouldn't interfere with his allopathic medicines. Instead, he would tell me that he wasn't giving in to his disease, that he was going to beat it. My contention was that if he wasn't willing to do something different to help himself, why would he expect to have different results?

During the time I knew him, I heard more about his lack of success with the healing process as being God's will.

I had to differ. God didn't stop him from trying different things. God didn't tell him to wear restrictive clothing that took him an eternity to put on and take off. He wasn't working a full-time job so I knew that God wasn't telling him that he couldn't rest when he felt tired. I also knew that God wasn't telling him to enter willfully into stressful situations. If this was really God's will, then God has a lot to answer for.

It has always seemed to me that God is always being blamed or credited for something. Every war from the Crusades onward has been fought in the name of God. It's amazing the way God seems to choose sides. If one side wins the war, the victor will say it was God's will. If one side loses the war, the loser will say it was God's will. It's akin to the nonsense I heard growing up that "this war will be the end of all wars." As a child, it never made sense to me. As an adult I see it as a bunch of gibberish because anyone with a lick of common sense knows that wars beget other wars; they don't end them.

This brings us to the heart of the matter: knowing when it's God's will or your will. If you have done everything that is humanly possible, and you keep doing everything that is humanly possible and it still isn't giving you the desired results, then maybe, just maybe, it's God's will.

On the other hand, if you allow yourself to feel defeated before you have exhausted every avenue at your disposal and it still hasn't yielded the desired results, then look inward and acknowledge that it's your will and not God's will that has deprived you of success.

And best of all, if it's your will that has sabotaged your success, you can change the outcome by changing yourself. If you make the effort to find the opportunity in every difficulty, you will be living in accordance with universal laws and overcoming every obstacle in your path.

CHAPTER 12
THINKING OUTSIDE THE BOX

Every time I hear someone talking about thinking outside the box, I wonder about the body that's being held prisoner inside the box.

If this were a case of astral traveling, astral projection, or bilocation, it would be understandable because we know that while the mind can be in one place, the body can be in another place.

There have been numerous documented cases of people undergoing surgery who have seen themselves on the ceiling looking down at their body on the table, watching everything that was being done to them and hearing everything that was being said.

While some of these astral projections are often brought about when a person is under anesthesia, there are numerous documented cases of people who are able to be in two places at one time during sleep or during meditation.

Have you ever had the experience of being asleep and feeling that you were falling and then your body jerks you awake? Your heart may be beating hard and there may be a feeling of disorientation. This has been described as a hard landing when the astral body comes back into your physical body as you're waking up.

It is not uncommon for a person deep in sleep to travel to other places. You see everything and hear everything and when you wake up, there is a vivid memory of it. I remember one such experience.

I had been corresponding with a prisoner as part of an outreach program called Over the Wall, through the Association for Research and Enlightenment (A.R.E.). Their mission is to help people change their lives for the better through the ideas and information found in the Edgar Cayce readings. (Cayce was the foremost psychic and medical clairvoyant of the twentieth century and his legacy lives on in over 14,000 readings on file at the A.R.E.).

One morning, just as I was waking up, but still in a dream state, I saw the boy I had been corresponding with. He was sleeping on a cot in a small cell with metal bars on the one small window and I heard the penetrating sound of metal clanging and banging against metal and a lot of loud voices. My heart was beating very fast and I woke up with a sudden start.

I looked at the clock, noted the time, and immediately wrote him a letter asking him about the occurrence. He wrote back saying that was breakfast being brought to the inmates' cells and the sounds I heard were the sounds he hears every morning.

I wrote another letter describing the boy sleeping on the cot and he told me that I had actually seen him because that's what he looks like. This was long before computers, emails, and Google so there were no pictures to download and only snail mail to verify what I had seen.

There is a correlation between thinking outside the box and the metaphysical occurrences I just described. Both of them call on the creativity of the mind, one during sleep and one during waking hours.

When you leave your mind open, in its receptive state, you are capable of thinking outside the box and getting answers to complex problems while you are awake or when you are sleeping or meditating. This means that you are also capable of being in two places at the same time because you are operating on different planes of consciousness in both instances.

Thinking outside the box actually requires you to suspend the thought process long enough for the answers to come into your mind. Most people are so busy thinking that they don't allow their minds to be quiet enough to receive the answers.

People who meditate have the advantage because they have learned how to quiet the mind. They have also discovered that while you can't meditate and think at the same time, you can meditate and be somewhere else at the same time. This allows you to find solutions to problems from a higher plane of consciousness, otherwise known as thinking outside the box.

CHAPTER 13
A GHOST INSIDE HIM OR A PAST LIFE MEMORY?

From time to time we hear of a child who has vivid memories of a lifetime that can't be explained by normal phenomena. That's the case of four-year-old Andrew Lucas who cries hysterically as he asks his mother, "Why did you let me die in that fire?"

His mother, Michele, says he is saying things and recalling memories that no one his age should know. She has become so scared that a ghost might be inhabiting her son's body, that she went online and did some extensive research about the things Andrew was telling her, namely that his name was U.S. marine Sgt. Val S. Lewis and he was killed in a terrorist bomb attack in Beirut.

She came across a TV show, *Ghost Inside My Child* and "the producers of the show helped the Lucas family connect the information provided from Andrew to a group of marines who died in the 1983 bomb blast in Lebanon decades before Andrew was born."

The Lucas family decided to go to the grave where Sgt. Lewis was buried to see if Andrew could put his memories to rest. Andrew went right up to the grave and he put the flowers down, and then he ran to another grave and it was a marine and he said, "That's my friend."

Andrew's parents had hoped that if Andrew came face-to-face with his past life, his memories would disappear. This hasn't happened and his parents are very worried about him. They don't know if they should be scared that a ghost has invaded his body or if this is something that a psychic can help them with.

In 1966, Ian Stevenson, M.D., wrote a book, *Twenty Cases Suggestive of Reincarnation*, in which he documents cases of children who remembered their past lives vividly.

56 • A SOUL'S GUIDE TO METAPHYSICS AND SPIRITUALITY

This was at a time when psychic phenomena was not widely known and he was presenting his research which he personally investigated, reported on, and discussed in the *Proceedings* of the American Society for Psychical Research. He was very careful to say that these cases were suggestive of reincarnation, not that they proved the case for reincarnation, although the cases were mostly verified by Dr. Stevenson, himself.

A lot has happened since Stevenson's book first came out. If I were Andrew's parents, I'd investigate this past life more thoroughly and help him integrate the lessons of his past life with his four-year-old present life until new memories allow him to let go of the past.

CHAPTER 14
WAKING UP IN SOMEONE ELSE'S BODY

What would you do if you woke up from a coma in someone else's body, speaking a foreign language?

Rory Curtis, a twenty-five-year-old British man, was in a coma for six days following a horrific car accident on a busy motorway in England. He suffered extensive brain damage; his blood vessels had burst and blood was leaking into his brain. For six days, doctors battled round the clock to save his life. When he woke up, he was speaking fluent French and he believed he was Hollywood A list actor, Matthew McConaughey.

Rory described the moment he looked in the mirror and saw someone else looking back at him. He said, "I didn't know what I was looking at." During his time in the hospital he was thinking that he couldn't wait to get out of the hospital and go back to filming movies. Eventually, everything clicked into place and he realized that he wasn't Matthew McConaughey.

Rory has now retrained as a barber and he is learning to teach hairdressing. I know if I had been in his shoes, and I had believed that I was an A-list actor, I would have figured that I was being given a second chance and that this was a sign that I was supposed to train as an actor.

But what would you do if you really did wake up from a coma in someone else's body? Although it sounds like a science fiction plot of a movie, with so many things being discovered that were never known before, it's not entirely out of the realm of possibility.

There is so much about the brain that we do not know. Scientists have suppositions but no conclusions. How did Rory wake up speaking fluent French when he hadn't studied it since the ninth grade and, by his own admission, he wasn't a good student? Supposedly, you don't learn something new; you just speak with a foreign accent.

But that isn't the case with Rory. He *is* doing something new; he is speaking fluent French when scientists had agreed that people wouldn't be learning anything new.

He has a chance at a new life. What are the odds that he's going to use this opportunity for the betterment of mankind? It would seem such a shame if he didn't make radical changes to reflect his "awakening."

CHAPTER 15
PAST LIVES AND FUTURE LIVES

More and more people are accepting the possibility that we have lived before and that the universal law of karma does exist. Many people have been hypnotized into a previous life and have gone on to write books about their past life experiences.

Now that scientists are getting interested in the concept of time travel, they are saying that using Einstein's theory of relativity, we will be able to go into the future, but traveling back in time may not be possible. My thought has always been that if you can go forward in time, there must be a way to go back in time.

There have been numerous paranormal books exploring the concept of finding wormholes that allow you to go back in time. Some of them have come up with the theory that these wormholes only stay open for a limited time so, if you travel back to a previous lifetime and you want to come back to the present lifetime, you have to know how much time you have in which to make that roundtrip journey.

But, this brings up the law of karma. If we can travel back in time, can we correct our mistakes in a previous life so that we don't reap the negative karma in this life from our dissolute actions of the past? In other words, if we really can go back in time and correct our mistakes, and find the wormhole to bring us back to this lifetime, will our negative karma be erased as if it had never existed?

Following that line of questioning, we would have to look at a different part of the karmic picture. We have all experienced some kind of déjà vu, the strong feeling that you have already seen or experienced something. Therefore, it is reasonable to think that we might have been looking into our own future.

If, indeed, we are capable of seeing our own future, can we not also manipulate the law of karma so that we know what to expect and thus, be able to circumvent the hardships associated with negative karma?

For those of us who like thinking about "what if" scenarios, the possibilities are infinite and worth pondering.

CHAPTER 16
A SURREAL EXPERIENCE

I just had a surreal experience and if I hadn't been with my friend when it happened, I would have thought I had dreamed it or imagined it.

Several days ago, I wrote about calling a restaurant that my friend and I had decided to try. The woman who answered the phone told me what was on the menu and the prices. When I asked for the address and directions to the restaurant, I gave the phone to my friend because he was the one driving.

The address I was given was different from the address this same woman gave my friend, as were the landmarks. We ended up at a completely different restaurant that had nowhere near the variety of foods that the woman had told me about. We were hungry so we ate there rather than driving around trying to find the other place.

I struggled over whether to phone the owner of the first restaurant and then I came to the decision that if I were the owner of that restaurant, I would want to know if one of my employees was telling my customers to go elsewhere. So, I decided to call the restaurant and speak to the owner. And here's where it gets surrealistic.

I had gone online to find a restaurant near us and found one that looked interesting. They had a wide assortment of foods with pictures of them. They all looked mouthwatering and very different from the usual fare. I noted the address and called them.

When I went back to the website, the name of the restaurant was the same and the phone number was the same, but everything else was different. I called and asked if they had one of the meals I had wanted to try and they said no. I asked if they had ever had that item and they said no, they had always had the same items and those were the only things they ever advertised.

Then I looked at all the restaurants on that page, and I know it was the same page because all of it looked familiar. The only thing that was different was the menu. That was radically different and not the least appealing. I called all of the restaurants on that page and none of them had ever carried the kinds of foods that were on the other menu.

If it weren't for the fact that my friend was with me and shared this experience, I'd have thought that I had imagined the whole thing.

CHAPTER 17
NOTHING IS HOPELESS

Nothing is hopeless. No matter how often people or circumstances try to crush the human spirit, with the least little bit of hope it springs back to life.

We see this trait in revolutionaries. No matter how tired they are and how hopeless their cause seems to be, when they see the smallest glimmer of hope, they reach inside of themselves for that extra burst of energy and that extra ounce of determination and continue fighting.

We have seen people who have been beaten down by life, who have given up and don't care if they live or die, but as soon as they sense that someone is reaching out to help them, they find the strength to rise up and grab that help with both hands.

And that makes me think that nothing is really hopeless. I have often said that you have to know when to let go of something, that maybe if you have tried your best and it still hasn't happened, that maybe it's not meant to be, and this is certainly a rule I have lived by. But now that I'm writing about the possibility of nothing being hopeless, I'm starting to wonder if I shouldn't rethink that rule.

In retrospect, the principle of knowing when to stop pushing the river because it flows by itself, has saved me a lot of time, energy, and wasted emotion. But if we can constantly keep being revived with just a little bit of hope and determination, then maybe I should keep pushing that river and see where else I can get it to flow.

Another one of my precepts has always been to choose my battles carefully because I can't fight on every front. This was a very important realization for me because when I was young, I used to fight for everything that I thought was important. And when I was young, *everything* was important.

Nowadays, I try to limit myself to just fighting for my principles whereas in my younger days, I fought for every cause that I thought bordered on an injustice. I still fight injustice but I choose my battles more carefully.

I have learned not to be the maverick of lost causes, or at least I've *tried* to learn not to be the maverick of lost causes. For one thing, there are so many of these lost causes that I know it's impossible to fight for all of them. For another thing, I don't have the energy of my younger years to fight for all of them.

They say that age makes you mellow. Nah. Age just makes you more tired so you don't have the energy to expend on all battle fronts. And that's probably more to the point of why you need to choose your battles carefully because you can't stay young forever, even if nothing is really hopeless.

CHAPTER 18
DO YOU BELIEVE IN MIRACLES?

I don't think I have ever heard so many stories about miracles as I've heard in the last ten years. In fact, I could probably count them on one hand until recently.

About forty years ago, a woman who had been diagnosed as completely paralyzed by every specialist in the county, and gone through every test available at the time, was the first time I witnessed a miracle. For all the years I knew her, she was dependent on her husband to take her everywhere, always pushing her in the wheelchair.

One day, they were in their apartment and she saw her husband fall down and die, right in front of her. The shock was so great that it must have triggered something in her. She got up and put her wheelchair away, and never used it again. She was no longer paralyzed.

Now we hear of people who have been in a coma suddenly waking up and remembering everything up to the moment when they went into a coma. One woman had been in a coma for five years and the first words out of her mouth was "I want to go to a Bob Seger concert."

We keep hearing stories about people who have been pronounced dead, waking up at their own funeral. Most of the time there are happy endings to that story but one man was so shocked, that he died of a heart attack at his own funeral.

Not that long ago, a woman gave birth to twins and one of them was stillborn. The doctor told her that the girl made it but the boy died. She took the boy into her bed and for two hours, she hugged him, touched him, told him she loved him and, all of a sudden, he started to move. He and his sister are both alive and well.

There are countless stories about people being in a coma for years and suddenly waking up. Some of them wake up speaking a foreign language and some wake up with a skill they had never had before. Recently, a premature baby who was thought to be dead, was buried and, when her father dug her up, she started to breathe.

We hear of people going into comas every day. Some of them last for decades and then they suddenly wake up. We hear of comatose people being declared brain dead, MRIs showing no brain activity for months on end, and then they suddenly wake up and they can talk and recognize people.

So, when I'm asked if I believe in miracles, my answer is, "I sure do. Where there is life, there's hope and, sometimes, where there isn't life, there is still hope."

CHAPTER 19
IS THERE A REASON FOR EVERYTHING?

I have always heard that there is a reason for everything. First from deeply religious people who have endured tragedy and didn't know why and then, when I got older, when I studied metaphysics and learned about the law of karma.

We like to think our suffering is for a reason; why then, do these terrible things happen to us if there isn't a reason? So we accept terms like it's God's will or, as you sow, so shall you reap. What goes around, comes around, universal laws, laws of retribution or retributive karma. It may not make sense to us if we can only accept what our five senses perceive but, for most people, it's better than nothing.

The French poet and novelist, Anatole France, had a different belief system; he said, "Men are born; they suffer; they die."

When it comes to wars, national and international strife, natural disasters, etc., you would have to believe in the law of karma to see the correlation between past actions and present punishment or rewards. Some people would say that the law of karma obviates free will while others would say that you have free will, but it's on a very short leash.

We're living in a very different world; there are much fewer deeply religious people than ever before.

Nowadays, people want real answers; they don't want to hear it's God's will or there is a reason for everything. They want to make sense of their lives. They want to have some control over their lives.

We tell our children to study hard, go to college, and doors will magically open for you. And for those who do study hard and get a good education, too many graduates are finding that there is no magic door that opens for them and they are just as unemployable as those who got no further than high school.

While health care has improved since the Middle Ages, more people than ever before are getting incurable diseases and we still don't know why, let alone have cures for the worst of them.

Although I'm a strong reincarnationist and I have accepted the law of karma because it explains so much, I'm still left to wonder if maybe there aren't some mistakes that occur randomly, like maybe the huge pit in an avocado.

CHAPTER 20
BEYOND BELIEF

There has been enough documentation of people having the ability to communicate with animals, that I tend to believe that man has that ability.

I've seen videos of animals doing some remarkable things that show their intelligence and their communication skills and I doubt if those videos were doctored. I can even imagine someone having the ability to communicate with an animal's soul immediately after it dies. But, here's where I draw the line.

A woman was recounting her experience in a clothing store. It was bitter cold outside and she had just left a warm climate and wasn't prepared for the cold weather. When she looked at the coats on display, a fox coat caught her eye. She wanted it. But she was a strong animal rights advocate.

The way she told the story is that she walked over to this fox coat and started talking to the dead animal. She explained that she was very cold and needed the warmth of the coat and hoped that the fox would pardon her for buying it.

And here's where I mentally drew the line: She then went on to say that she communicated with the fox's spirit and it told her that it was glad she was going to get the warmth she needed from the coat and she had its permission to buy the coat and to enjoy its warmth.

My mind shut down at that point and I thought Oooo Kaaay. You're not only communicating with an animal that's been dead a long time, but you're communicating with an animal that's been tanned and sewed into a coat.

I'm a strong believer in the afterlife and I think that certain people are able to pierce the veil that separates our material world from the spiritual world. But communicating with an animal that is not only dead, but has also been tanned and sewed, is stretching my level of credulity beyond the bounds of my fertile imagination.

Nonetheless, I'll keep an open mind to the extent that I won't shut the door on it but I'm willing to revisit it if there is evidence to support it.

For now, I'll stick to the belief that many people have the ability to communicate with live animals, and leave it at that.

CHAPTER 21
MY LIFE IN A FORTUNE COOKIE

I'm not usually given to looking for signs from the universe to guide me in my daily decisions but, for a very brief period of time, that's exactly what I did.

It all began, many years ago, when I went to a Chinese restaurant with a couple of friends. We were having a lovely evening and eating our way to Nirvana when the waitress came over and gave us our Fortune cookies.

I usually smile when I read the superficial sayings in the Fortune cookies but that night, all three of us received messages that were meaningful. My friends were told things about their careers, all of them true and all of them significant. My fortune told of a trip that I would be taking and, it too, was true. My hotel and plane reservations had already been booked and my speaking engagement had already been confirmed. And everything it said, proved to be true.

From then on, and for many months after, I managed to go to a Chinese restaurant at least once a month so that I could get my Fortune cookie. And if I couldn't get out to go to the restaurant, I had a meal delivered. It didn't matter whether the meal was good as long as I got my Fortune cookie.

For the next several months, my universe seemed to be contained in a Fortune cookie and I kept looking for signs that I was on the right path. There's nothing like the power of the mind to convince you that if you just open one more cellophane-wrapped cookie, you would know what all your tomorrows would bring.

Needless to say, a few months later, my cookie message was so trite that it didn't bear thinking about. At first, I toyed with the idea of asking the waitress to bring me another Fortune cookie so that I could get a different message, but then I thought that if I was meant to have a more meaningful message, I would have had one.

The next few times were just as unproductive; all the messages went back to being superficial and meaningless, so I stopped going to Chinese restaurants.

I guess my lesson in all of this was that I needed to go more deeply within, via my meditations, and not depend on external sources for guidance. And that was the end of my Fortune cookie caper.

CHAPTER 22
MORNING THOUGHTS

I read an interesting article about how you should start your day with beautiful, loving thoughts. The author talked about taking a few minutes as you wake up to think about things that are pleasurable.

I don't know about him but, many of us wake up with an intense need to relieve our bladder and, by the time we're walking out of the bathroom, our minds are filled with our regular thoughts.

Then, too, many people wake up to the sound of a jarring alarm that would destroy anyone's peaceful dreams or thoughts, and other people wake up to the insistent ringing of the telephone. By the time the call ends or the alarm has been turned off, you can forget about your intentions to slowly open your eyes to positive and calming thoughts to send you on your way to a tranquil day.

The author also forgets that some people are morning people and others are night people. If you are a night person and grouchy in the morning, you won't be thinking about taking a few minutes to embrace those positive thoughts. You'll be thinking that you want to go back to sleep and positive thoughts be damned.

Then there are morning people, many of whom jump out of bed, ready to start the day as soon as they open their eyes. They usually don't want to waste a minute of their morning, thinking that this is their most productive time of the day. Perhaps some of them will take a few minutes to try to pull in those positive thoughts but most of them will be too anxious to start their day as soon as they wake up.

If the real world didn't intrude, the author might have had a good point about using those first few minutes of the day to immerse yourself in positive and loving thoughts. However, in light of how people really start their day, this seems like a fantasy.

Meditation seems a more practical approach. It doesn't matter where or when a person meditates; if he meditates every day, he will start to feel that inner sense of peace all the time. He won't have to change his routine or his way of submerging himself into a serene state of being; it will be on tap for him all the time.

CHAPTER 23
THE LANGUAGE OF TENT REVIVALS

Many years ago, I watched a demonstration of one of the leading tent revival preachers of his day show his audience how they get people to open their wallets to give large donations. He said that, contrary to popular belief, it isn't so much the words they use as in the cadence of the words.

He walked up and down the aisle, addressing all five-hundred people in the studio audience, and pointed out the cadence that he was using to get people to part with their money. He even showed how they emphasized words to a certain beat and you're so caught up in the tempo that you scarcely hear the words.

Then, the most amazing thing happened. The cameras panned to the audience and, as he was making his pitch for donations, you could see women reach for their purses and men reach for their wallets.

At the time, I was teaching a course in parapsychology, so that week I told my class about this preacher and I said that I would demonstrate what I had seen.

Using the same cadence that he used, I told my class that they needed to make an appointment with me for a counseling session. I kept the words and the message simple and I mimicked the cadence that he used. As soon as I finished with my pitch, every single student told me they wanted to make an appointment with me for a counseling session.

I was flabbergasted. I kept saying, "No, no, no. I was only demonstrating the way tent revival preachers get people to part with their money. I wasn't trying to get you to make an appointment with me."

No matter how often I told them that this was just a demonstration and that I wasn't really asking them to come for an appointment, they wouldn't hear of it. Almost as one, they each made an appointment for a counseling session.

It was the most amazing thing I had ever seen. It was almost like mass hypnosis. I thought surely, when they got home, they would realize that they didn't need to make an appointment and they would cancel out. Instead, the phone stayed silent and each student, before leaving their session, told me they didn't realize how much they needed that appointment.

They didn't want to believe it was just the cadence.

CHAPTER 24
DREAMING IN COLOR

My dreams have always played an important part of my life. The really meaningful ones are in color and leave memories that are too vivid to forget. They are the ones that prompt me to think about a situation in ways that I hadn't considered before and to take whatever action is needed, even when I hadn't realized that an action was needed.

When we hear terms like thinking outside the box, most people are tapping into their unconscious mind where their dreams reside. It's the hidden part of a person and probably the most interesting part of a person because it's not affected by the opinions of society or of one's family and friends.

The most creative people in the world are those who tap into their dreams for their ideas. Sometimes it seems as though they are staring into space, accomplishing nothing but the reality is that this is their most productive time.

President Jimmy Carter and his wife, Rosalynn, were both writing books. The president is one of those people who can sit down and start to write. His wife is not one of those people.

One day, the president walked past their bedroom and saw Rosalynn lying on the bed, staring into space. He said, "I thought you were writing a book" and she said, "I am." What her husband didn't realize was that although it looked like she was staring into space and accomplishing nothing, she was actually tapping into that hidden part of her, the unconscious mind, for her creative ideas.

I loved Rosalynn Carter's book, *First Lady from Plains*, and it was a national bestseller, which just goes to prove that the time she spent staring into space was worth every second of her active/passive writing style. I call it an active/passive writing style because she is actively writing about something in a passive way.

This active/passive style is also how I would classify meditation. To meditate effectively, you cannot pursue it aggressively; you have to clear your mind of all thoughts and let it come to you.

This, then, is the essence of spirituality; it is the pathway to your higher consciousness where perfection resides. By tapping into your unconscious mind, the repository of your creative ideas, you are also tapping into the beginning of the soul's quest for perfection.

CHAPTER 25
DO YOU BELIEVE IN AFFIRMATIONS?

When I first started studying the principles of metaphysics, I kept hearing about the power of affirmations. I looked around at the people who believed in them so strongly and I couldn't see where the use of their affirmations had helped them.

If my back hurt, it hurt, and no amount of affirmations that my back was healed, or that I was completely healthy, or that I lived in perfect health and wellbeing, made the pain go away.

This was no different than hearing people affirming to the universe that they were good. They would reaffirm, at all times of the day and night, that they lived in God-consciousness, and they acted from their higher self. In theory, this sounded very lovely, In actuality, it was a bunch of rubbish.

These same people, having affirmed how good they are and how spiritual they are, then went on to cheat people out of money, pilfer their time and energy without recompense, lie, treat employees or other underlings unkindly, take advantage of others in a variety of ways. and live their lives no differently than if they hadn't spouted all those affirmations.

It has long been my belief that if you were sitting in the middle of a dark room and affirming, "The light will go on. The light will go on. The light will go on," nothing would happen unless you got up and turned the light on.

The same is true of saying things like "I am a good person. I am very spiritual. I live in my higher self." Until you modify your behavior to match those affirmations, nothing will change; you will be no closer to God-consciousness than you were before you said all those things.

If you want to change the status of anything in your life, you have to change your actions to match your intentions.

Intent is the first step. Commitment is the second step. And action is the last step. When you have done this, your heart, mind, and body will be in perfect alignment and you will be living a spiritual life.

CHAPTER 26
PUSHING THE ENVELOPE

When I was in college, I read a poem by Emily Dickinson that spoke of those who had not lived while they were alive and, only in their death, did they become alive. It was one of those poems that made me look at the life I was living and this was a turning point in my thinking.

After I thought about it, I decided that I was going to fill my days with the things that gave meaning to my life. It didn't have to meet with anyone's approval or standards for how my life should be lived. In fact, I told no one about it. I didn't want anyone else's opinions to cloud my decision. I wanted to do this for me.

So there I was, in my mid-teens, making a decision for how I was going to live the rest of my life. I made a commitment to learn something new every day, even if it was only looking up a new word in the dictionary and using it in sentences all day. And, except for the days when I was sick, I've managed to do that.

I also decided to take emotional risks. As long as no one knew about this commitment to my personal development, I felt comfortable setting this as a goal. And one of those emotional risks was trying to overcome whatever obstacles were in my life, which, to this day, is always terrifying at the beginning.

Phobias are extremely difficult to overcome and I didn't attempt to overcome my largest one until well into middle age. It was my acrophobia (a fear of heights) that almost did me in. I gave myself different assignments to help me deal with it.

I made myself go up in a few helicopters (ugh!! it was horrible). And I made myself climb a pyramid (even worse than the helicopter rides), and then I made myself accomplish the goal I had set for myself which was standing on an eight-foot ladder to put an ornament on top of my fourteen-foot-Christmas tree.

That was as much as I was willing to do to confront my acrophobia. The assignments I gave myself never got easier and I'm not a glutton for punishment; I decided to quit while I was ahead. But I still push the envelope because I don't want to think I was already dead while I was still alive.

CHAPTER 27
A WOMAN WORTH KNOWING

Michelle Puckett is in the business of giving help to people who are the victims of circumstance. She has a unique consignment store that sells designer clothes and accessory items from quality designers, like Chanel, Gucci and Ferragamo, for 80 percent below cost but she also has a nonprofit for people who have been out of work and are struggling to get their lives back on track.

In addition to her consignment shop, she started a nonprofit to help victims of domestic violence and senior citizens by lending clothing for job interviews and offering résumé services. The clothes come from both donations and the consignment store, and they're returned after use.

Her nonprofit has provided assistance to 148 disadvantaged and battered women, 22 struggling men and around 87 senior citizens, and nursing homes. She also provides disadvantaged women from local shelters with "Baskets of New Life" which contain hair products, makeup, jewelry and other accessories to help these women find a fresh start.

Anyone who has ever been out of work and out of money knows how depressing life can be. If you're lucky and get a job interview, there is the problem of what to wear. For those women who have been battered and living in shelters, safety has to come first and everything else comes after that.

Most of these women, if they are lucky enough to be able to escape a violent relationship, are usually not lucky enough to be able to leave with clothing that makes them look successful for the business world. And that's where Michelle Puckett's nonprofit comes in. Through this arm of her business, she breathes new life and hope into people who have lost all hope for a decent life.

Many women don't feel dressed for success unless they are wearing makeup and jewelry. They can be wearing the most expensive designer outfit but unless their hair is styled nicely and they are wearing makeup, they lack the confidence to interview well. Puckett knows this and that's why she gives these "Baskets of New Life" to these women.

Puckett's goal is to build her nonprofit and have people come in and shop, consign, and donate. Her compassion and sense of community definitely makes her a woman worth knowing.

CHAPTER 28
THERE'S NO SUCH THING AS ESP?

I used to think that research studies meant something but the criteria that is being used by some Australian researchers to debunk ESP, are just plain silly.

The ESP study, which is led by Dr Piers Howe from the Melbourne School of Psychological Sciences, University of Melbourne, has concluded that there is no such thing as sixth sense. They used a criteria that is not too dissimilar from the playing cards that were used many decades ago to debunk psychic ability, by having the participants guess what cards they were holding.

Dr. Howe's participants were shown two portrait color photos of a female and asked participants to identify the change they saw after switching the photos at timed intervals. They were asked to identify the change by having them click one out of nine possible options in a list, e.g., earrings, glasses, hat, necklace, color of lipstick, etc.

Their conclusion was that the results prove that the observers could generally identify when a change had occurred even when they could not identify exactly what it was. They are calling this ability "Mindsight" and saying that Mindsight is the ability to detect changes before being able to identify them.

I don't know what they were researching but it certainly wasn't ESP. Ask any parent who has ever sensed his or her child in danger, even from thousands of miles away, if those feelings were the result of detecting changes before being able to identify it.

In the days before Caller ID, whenever a particular friend would call, I would drive him crazy by picking up the phone and saying, Hi, Simon, before he could identify himself. There also were many times I would think about someone and within minutes to hours that person would call, even if I hadn't spoken to her or him in five years.

It's also the ability to sense danger before it happens. My friend and I had decided to go to a particular restaurant and, just as we got there, I made her drive past it and go somewhere else. The evening news that night reported that robbers came into that restaurant when we would have been there and held everyone up at gunpoint, going from table to table collecting money and jewels and roughing up some people who didn't hand over their valuables fast enough.

Those weren't changes that the mind could detect before being able to identify them. That was ESP.

CHAPTER 29
THAT OLD TIME RELIGION

I was talking to a friend today about religion. Usually, I avoid talking about religion because so many hard feelings erupt from those kinds of discussions but today I made an exception because of some of the comments he made.

He was telling me that the membership at his place of worship has dropped considerably, and those who are members, some of them give donations but don't attend services. He said that even the donations have dropped considerably.

I look at the religious groups around the country and I can see the same thing happening everywhere. It's not just his religious group; it's everyone's religious group. What's the reason?

For one thing, religion is based on emotion, and large numbers of religious people aren't getting drawn into their religions the way they used to. For another thing, in the old days, people congregated at their houses of worship during the week as their social club. Nowadays, people are so tied into their electronic devices, they don't have the time or the inclination to devote to religious pursuits; they would much rather chat on their cell phone or use their iPad, or surf the Internet.

The underlying reason for people leaving their religion, centers mostly around the fact that their leaders are still preaching that old time religion without taking into account that lifestyles have undergone massive changes while religion hasn't changed at all.

In the old days, religion was all about emotion and guilt trips, especially if you didn't feel like going to services. Today, with so many things pulling people in all directions, if religion is to survive in a big way, they have to understand the behavior of their members and how today's society is very different from the society of yesteryear.

Then, too, religion has been polarizing this country in such a negative way that it's not leaving people with a good feeling about themselves, their neighbors, or their religion. There have always been different ideologies but people seemed more accepting of different beliefs than they are today.

So, once again, religion is not dealing with the behavioral changes that have been taking place in society.

If religious leaders want to bring more people into their fold, they need to make them feel more spiritual by attending services, not stand in judgment of those whose beliefs are different from their own. They need to touch their hearts before they touch their wallets.

CHAPTER 30
I'M ONLY HUMAN

What happened to accountability? In the old days, we knew that we were responsible for our actions and that every action had a consequence. Have the times changed so much that this is no longer true? And more important, why are we accepting a standard of mediocrity instead of a standard of excellence?

Wherever I go, I hear people saying, "I'm only human" as an excuse for doing something that they know they shouldn't have done or for not doing something that they said they would do. In the business world this can be deadly. If a team member drops the ball his team may not reach its goals and the company may not survive these economic hard times.

I have been watching one of the major airlines for the last several years. Their customer service has been atrocious; no one has taken accountability for their actions and one of the employees at the executive level even made the comment, "I'm doing the best I can but I'm only human."

Interestingly enough, this airline, which used to be ranked as one of the best, is now in such deep financial trouble that the only way they can survive is if they merge with a more profitable airline.

Businesses are having problems with the mediocrity of many of their employees who don't feel compelled to do an honest day's work for an honest day's pay. Many of them take advantage of their employers by spending their days texting and emailing their friends during regular business hours, or posting their personal comments on social networking sites. And many of these posters have been fired from their jobs because of it.

One such employee posted his picture with his friends at a bar and bragged that he had just called in sick to his office. His employer saw the picture and comments and when this man came to work the next day, he was fired.

We seem to be fostering a nation of self-indulgent people who feel they are entitled to the best of everything while working as little as possible. Employees used to be proud of their work; now they need bigger and better bonuses and rewards systems to do the job they were hired to do. We have become so accustomed to mediocrity that when an employee does his job, we shower him with gratitude.

We all have busy workloads but if we commit to doing something, we should just do it, even if we have to work round the clock to get it done. It's not acceptable to shrug our shoulder and say, "Sorry. I had so much to do that I couldn't get to it; I'm only human."

How do you feel when you are expecting a call and it doesn't come or you have an appointment with someone who neither shows up nor calls you with an explanation? Or worse, still... when they take a cavalier attitude and give you some lame excuse and then say in their defense, "I'm only human." These words have become so pervasive, that it has become the rallying cry of the self-indulgent members of society.

I once read a complaint by an employee who felt it was unfair of her employer to fire her for being late for work every day. She said that after numerous latenesses and being written up by her supervisor for many months on end, her employer had given her one last chance to redeem herself. If she came to work on time every day for the next six months, she could keep her job and the documentation concerning her tardiness would be expunged.

A few weeks later her babysitter got sick and couldn't come to her house. She called her office to say she would be coming in late but that she would be there as soon as she got another sitter. When she showed up two hours later, she was fired on the spot.

Her employer told her that she showed a lack of good judgment: if she had just taken the day off as one of her personal days or one of her sick days, she could have kept her job. She could even have kept her job if she showed up for work on time with her child and left it up to her supervisor to either let her child stay there for the day or let her go home and find another babysitter before coming back.

The employee's contention was that when she called to say that she would be late, she should have been told what the consequences would be. She signed her complaint "I'm only human."

There are many times when it is appropriate to say, "I'm only human" but those occasions are limited to when you have tried to do everything within your power to accomplish something and it still remains beyond your reach.

A perfectionist might need to learn how to say, "I'm only human" when things are beyond his control, but it's sad to hear people uttering these words when they haven't made much of an effort to fulfill a commitment, to change their behavior, or to accomplish their goal.

CHAPTER 31
OUR CHANGING VALUES

In our family, we always heard that a person's word is his bond and that you're as good as your word. We also lived by the creed that a deal can be sealed with a handshake. Years later, with the changing values, people were advised to seal their deals in writing and in an attorney's office.

We seemed to live in simpler times where white hats represented the good guys and black hats represented the bad guys. You could identify the bad guys because they always looked bad. They were dressed in sleazy clothes, smelled bad, and were poorly educated.

In today's society, those same bad guys are dressed in Armani suits, wearing a Rolex watch and some woodsy cologne, and quite possibly are Ivy League graduates.

I take promises very seriously. If I promise to do something, I do it. If I promise to not do something, I don't do it. End of story. Therefore, I make it my business to not promise anything that I might not be able to fulfill. And even worse, if someone promises me something, I expect them to come through with it. When that fails to happen, my respect for that person plummets by several notches and I know not to believe anything they tell me.

Harsh. But there you have it. That's how I was brought up and I've never been able to break away from what I learned at my parents' knees.

Stress has been blamed for a lot of things, e.g., rudeness, breaking promises, theft, quitting a job or ending a relationship by email or by texting, continually breaking appointments or being late for appointments, etc., but what it boils down to is really a lack of character. When a person is under a lot of stress, that is the time when we get to see a person's true character.

It's easy to talk about the importance of integrity but it's not so easy to live it. If it isn't a soul-deep commitment, it crumbles under adversity. There are a couple of old axioms: "talk is cheap" and "actions speak louder than words." There have been a lot of jokes like "whoever says that talk is cheap has never had to pay a telephone bill", but not too many jokes have surfaced about actions speaking louder than words.

One of the most amazing assumptions that many people make is that they can do all sorts of nefarious things and, when called on the carpet, apologize for the act, be forgiven, and then repeat the same action with impunity. And why shouldn't they think they can do what they like if we let them get away with it?

I think each of us has a cutoff valve that tells us when enough is enough. Some people become abusive, shout, and storm off. Others retreat behind a wall of silence and lick their wounds in private. Some people express their feelings verbally or physically while others go into the passive-aggressive mode. But, for many others, they just avoid unpleasantness by pretending it doesn't exist or by avoiding the people who are causing it.

We seem to have lost our moral compass. We used to adhere to the Golden Rule: "Do unto others as you would have others do unto you." Nowadays, it seems as though people have adopted a new Golden Rule: "Do unto others before they do unto you" with the oft repeated mantra: "no good deed goes unpunished."

With accountability at an all-time low and people trying to see how much they can get away with, it's no wonder that scams are proliferating in a way they never have before. And even with proof that our actions come back to haunt us, people are still not able to connect the dots.

They still don't see that when you cheat someone, then someone will cheat you. When you betray someone, you can expect someone to betray you. When you take advantage of someone, you can almost predict that someone will take advantage of you. We see this precept in action every day and still there are so many who are oblivious to it and think it doesn't apply to them.

Life doesn't have to be so difficult. On the premise that we create our own hardships, we can also choose to create an easier life. For that to happen, we have to choose to live with kindness, dignity, and respect for all. We have to treat people as we would like to be treated.

CHAPTER 32
DEAF COMPOSER A FRAUD

We all know that many celebrities have ghost writers for their memoirs but their name appears on the cover along with the celebrity's name and it's all aboveboard. But this is the first time I ever heard of a ghost writer for musical compositions, letting his client take all the credit for his works and letting him be dubbed Japan's Beethoven.

The man who claimed to be the classical composer, Mamoru Samuragochi, also claimed that he is deaf, so his eighteen-year collaboration with Takashi Niigaki, a music teacher hired to write all his music, doesn't make sense.

According to Niigaki, Samuragochi isn't even deaf and his collaboration with him consisted of writing the music for him and sometimes playing them for him, and letting him choose which pieces he liked. My question is this: if Samuragochi is deaf, how did he listen to the music, let alone make the final selections?

This is a mammoth scam. Samuragochi had previously claimed to be the sole author of his classical works and sound tracks for video games such as Biohazard and his powerful "Hiroshima Symphony."

Samuragochi might never have confessed the truth had he not been worried that figure skater, Daisuke Takahashi, plans to use his arrangement, "Sonatina for Violin," at the Sochi Olympics and he feared that a disclosure of the truth later might be more awkward for him.

The magnitude of this fraud has rocked Japan's music industry and Nippon Columbia issued a statement expressing astonishment and outrage that Samuragochi had not composed his own music. The company stopped sales of his works, while major media outlets including national broadcaster NHK apologized for having run programs featuring Samuragochi as an accomplished composer.

When this brouhaha over Samuragochi's admission of having faked authorship of these compositions dies down, Japan and Nippon Columbia should be looking at promoting Takashi Niigaki as the musical virtuoso he is, and let him come out of the shadows of Samuragochi's undeserved fame.

CHAPTER 33
MODERN DAY DAVID AND GOLIATH

We're so accustomed to being passive when we run up against a force that is stronger than us that we cheer the little guy who takes on an airline.

It seems that an airline dumped a rabbi from its frequent flier club for complaining too much. This wasn't just someone who flew several times a month; this was someone who was a valued customer because he attained Platinum Elite status for flying 75,000 miles a year.

The airline claimed that the rabbi complained about service 24 times over eight months and that's why they took away his miles, rewards, and status. He said that they asked for his feedback and so he gave it.

He typically got perks like frequent flier miles and vouchers when he called, but not because he sought them, as the airline has claimed. He said he would call the airline and say, "This is my experience yesterday, and you asked for feedback, I'm giving it to you."

Usually before he was finished telling about his experience, they would interrupt him and say, "Well, as a gesture of goodwill, we're going to issue you either a couple thousand extra miles, or a voucher for some future travel."

The rabbi sued the airline for breach of contract. He said his suit is not about money; it's about courtesy. He said he wasn't complaining about too much salt on the peanuts, he was complaining about sitting on the tarmac for a few hours and no one giving information about why they were being delayed. He said that this shows a lack of decency, courtesy.

The rabbi's attorney argued that the airline did not act in good faith and said, "What's at stake for the average traveler is whether airlines have to perform their contracts in good faith, according to the reasonable expectations of the parties,"

Like a modern day David and Goliath, the rabbi got his hearing before the Supreme Court and said, "This was not a money thing; this was fighting for the rights of common citizens."

CHAPTER 34
ELDERLY FIRST-TIME MOTHERS

$$*$$

It seems that over the last decade, more and more women are talking about wanting babies but not being financially and emotionally ready for motherhood. They want to have their own biological baby someday but, they are afraid that if they wait until they are financially ready, they will be too old to conceive a child.

Most of these women can't afford to go to a fertility clinic to freeze their eggs when they are young, but now many companies are offering to pay for this option for career-minded women who will work for them during their reproductive years and use their frozen eggs when they are past childbearing age.

There have been many stories in the news lately about women in their sixties and seventies having their first child and it's almost becoming commonplace. Men have always been able to sire a child well into their dotage but I keep wondering about the moral implications of elderly people bringing a newborn into the world.

Although scientists are working on extending the lifespan of people to 150, it hasn't happened yet. There are thousands of people who are more than 100 years old, but they aren't starting a family at that age.

My question is one of ethics. Do we have the moral right to deliberately bring a child into the world when we're at an age when most of us will be sick or dying? If our bodies break down or we become mentally incompetent, who will raise that child and is it fair to the child or to the caretaker who will have to provide for the child?

Most old people don't have enough money put aside to set up a college fund for their children. Nor do they have enough money to clothe and feed a newborn for years to come.

If they are lucky and have planned their retirement well, they have just enough money to live out the rest of their years without having to resort to eating cat food.

Who will take care of this child when the parents die? And we will all die, some sooner and some later, but we will all die before this newborn reaches adulthood. Is it morally fair to bring a newborn into the world, knowing that you won't be there to watch him graduate from high school?

CHAPTER 35
TWO SIDES TO THE STORY

A woman who left her young children in a sweltering car while she went on a job interview attracted sympathy from around the country with a tear-stained mug shot after being arrested on felony child-abuse charges.

People responded to her plight to the tune of $114,000 in donations based on the fact that she was trying to get a job and was heartbroken when she realized she had endangered her children.

Prosecutors gave her a second chance by allowing her to keep her children and not face charges as long as she sets up a $60,000 trust fund for her children's education. She breached the deal by missing a Thursday deadline for putting money in the trusts, even after the amount of her payments was lowered to $40,000.

Now, she is being accused of spending most of the donated money. Prosecutors say that she has spent about $4,100 a month, including more than $1,000 in non-essentials such as cable TV, clothing and dining.

Of course, we're only getting one side of the story. She has small children. What if the clothing she bought was to replace clothing that her children had outgrown? She said that she didn't set up the education fund because she's concerned that her children won't have access to the money if they decide not to go to college.

For all we know, this woman may have heard stories about the huge administrative costs and legal fees that come out of trust funds and she may have felt that all the money would be eaten up by those expenses. The media didn't say whether she had access to a good accountant, financial planner, or attorney who was knowledgeable about those matters.

As for taking her children out for dinner, she says she isn't living an extravagant lifestyle by taking them to

McDonald's and Chuck E. Cheese, and she is still looking for work on a regular basis.

Perhaps her thinking skills aren't up to snuff, but that doesn't mean that she's stealing the donated money to fund a lavish lifestyle. It could be a case of not having enough information to make informed decisions about her spending.

When you're out of work and you have small children to feed and house, the world can be very frightening. So, maybe she didn't think too clearly that every dime she spends on restaurants and cable TV puts her one step closer to homelessness. Maybe she just needs someone to help her plan for their future.

CHAPTER 36

EXPOSED: GROOM-TO-BE FAKED HIS OWN DEATH

In this day and age when you have telephones, emails, and text messages to avoid difficult conversations, it's more than cowardly to fake your own death to avoid getting married; it's downright cruel.

The groom-to-be met his fiancée two years ago while she was studying abroad in the U.S. When she began making plans to return to England, he proposed and, during their daily calls, they began making plans to spend the rest of their lives together.

He wanted to be involved in the planning of their dream wedding so he said he booked the venue and they would be getting married on the campus where they met. She was ecstatic and couldn't think of a more romantic place to tie the knot.

Then, one week before he was supposed to be in England, she picked up her phone and heard a man's voice saying he was the father of her fiancé and that his son had been deeply depressed and wanted to die so he had thrown himself in front of a car. He said that they had been trying to send him for psychiatric care but it was too late.

She was devastated and, when she calmed down, she called his parents back to offer her condolences but they didn't know what she was talking about. They told her that their son was alive and well and he had told them that the two of them had broken up when she left the United States.

He later admitted that he had faked his own death because he was scared saying, "I'm a terrible, awful person. I know I shouldn't have told her I was dead, but I didn't know what else to do."

His fiancée has the right of it. She called him a liar and a coward, saying that he had put on a different voice on the phone and pretended to be his grieving father. She said, "What sort of sick person does that to his fiancée of two years? It's sickening."

In pretending to be his father and telling his fiancée that they had tried to get him to go for psychiatric care, he was probably telling her the only truth of their relationship . . . that he does, indeed, need psychiatric care.

I hope he gets professional help soon; he needs it desperately.

CHAPTER 37

THE HEIGHT OF IDIOCY

Did you ever do something really stupid and not even realize how stupid it was, especially with a whole community watching you? Well, that's what a 27-year-old pregnant woman did the other day but I don't now if she expected everyone in her small community to find out in such a public way.

The co-owner of a boutique was just returning to the store when he saw a woman leaving it in a hurry with an armload of clothing and jewelry. Suspecting it was a theft, he checked security footage which showed the theft taking place.

Two hours after the robbery, he saw pictures on Facebook of the woman wearing four of the boutique's stolen dresses, one of which was a neon, leopard pattern dress, which she was wearing on her updated profile picture.

He then posted a notice on Facebook telling of the robbery and showing her wearing the neon, leopard pattern dress. The post went viral. People from her community recognized her and called the police who arrested her.

Her only excuse after she was caught with her stash of clothing and jewelry was that there was nobody in there and that she could just take it. Apparently, she didn't know that they were in the back, working in the storeroom, and that if she was in that great a hurry to get home, she could have at least left a thank you note for making her stolen goods so readily accessible.

I guess I can understand how depressed she must have been feeling to have been reduced to stealing when she realized she was down to her last neon, leopard dress. I mean, how can you possibly exist with only one neon, leopard dress in your closet?

At this point, she may be regretting her actions. Although she was released from jail on her own recognizance, she now has a police record and will either have to go to jail or pay a stiff fine and do community service, or all of the above.

The good news is that a lot of women saw the dress on the boutique's website and want to buy that dress or something similar.

As for the well-dressed, pregnant thief, instead of wearing her stolen neon leopard dress, she may have to trade it in for a prison uniform. Can we say, orange is the new black?

CHAPTER 38
HOLD ONTO YOUR WALLET

I try to give people the benefit of the doubt because everyone has a story, some sadder than others, but sad nonetheless. But, then, there are those who don't have a sad story to excuse their lack of integrity and those are the ones whose actions I find it difficult to overlook.

Some years ago, a man told me that he had borrowed a substantial sum of money from his grandfather and he had never made any attempt to repay his debt. He was earning a very good income and he was spending most of it on his personal entertainment. When I asked him why he didn't start paying his grandfather back, his cavalier attitude toward repayment threw me for a loop. And I knew that if anyone owed him money, he would not shrug it off nor would he forgive the debt.

Yesterday, I heard another story about a man who borrowed someone's car and was ticketed by a surveillance camera for speeding. He didn't pay the ticket and he didn't try to clear the owner's name by telling the police that he was the one who was driving the car, not the owner. And then, he had the nerve to ask the owner if he could borrow his car again.

I keep hearing stories like these. It was one thing to hear people shrug off their indebtedness to banks and stores with comments like, "They can afford it; they're big business" even though those debts are passed on to the rest of us. But, it's another thing altogether to see someone shrug off a personal debt as if it's of no importance.

They don't seem to care if they borrow money from their family and friends, knowing they have no intention of paying it back. And they certainly don't care if they borrow money from acquaintances or total strangers; they're treated just as shabbily.

Even if they have good jobs and are earning a good living, there seems to be a compulsion to just keep borrowing more and more. They don't even seem concerned when you tell them that you're not going to lend them another penny until they pay back what they owe you. They just move on to another person who hasn't heard that they're a deadbeat.

I guess this is another version of keep your friends close and your enemies closer, but keep your wallet out of sight.

CHAPTER 39
FIRED? LAID OFF? GET A VIRTUAL RÉSUMÉ

It must be a sign of the times because I've never seen so many scam artists as I've seen recently. There is now a company that provides phony job references to go with a phony career history. For a fee, they will create a phony website for a phony company, along with a phone number where a company representative is waiting to serve as your phony reference.

It's always been standard operating procedure that if you can do some of what an employer lists in a classified ad, you pad the résumé to make it look like you have all the work

136 • A SOUL'S GUIDE TO METAPHYSICS AND SPIRITUALITY

experience that's required. Most people do that and no one questions the ethics of the person submitting a padded résumé.

But, somehow, whether this company is operating within the grey area of the law or not, what they're doing feels very unethical.

Nowadays, it's almost imperative for professional people to have their own websites. And it's not unheard of to ask family and friends to write glowing testimonials for your website telling how wonderful you are and how you helped them and their business succeed beyond their wildest expectations. But it's another thing to make up phony businesses, employers, a work history, and have someone pose as a company representative who is waiting to serve as your phony reference.

"The site describes itself as a utility for job seekers who have been rendered unemployable by firings or long gaps in their résumé. To hear them say it, they're providing an important service to those stigmatized by the blight of unemployment."

While I have the utmost compassion for people who have been fired or laid off, and I can understand why they feel they have been unfairly stigmatized by their unemployment, there is a very fine line between exaggerating a truth and outright lying.

Even if this company never gets caught and prosecuted for committing fraud, what they're doing still violates a personal sense of honor. I know these are hard times and it's horrendous to be out of work and not be able to meet your bills but there must be other ways to put food on the table without losing one's integrity.

CHAPTER 40
DEATHBED PROMISES

One of the most unfair promises that you'll ever be asked to make is a deathbed promise. It's usually such an emotional time as it is, to witness a loved one dying before your eyes and, pleading with you to honor their dying wish, places a burden of enormous magnitude on you.

I usually consider a promise a sacred trust, to be honored at all costs, but, after hearing some unreasonable dying wishes forced on people, I think I would have to exclude the ones made as the loved one is taking his last gasping breath.

In most relationships, people talk about the things that are important to them. They may not agree with one another, but at least their views on a subject have been discussed. If you don't want to be put in an unfair position at the end of a loved one's life, have as many of those discussions as you can and, if you don't want to be responsible for what's being asked of you, make it abundantly clear before it becomes a deathbed promise you're being asked to make.

Many people have said that the person was having such a hard time letting go, and they wanted him or her to go peacefully, so they agreed to do whatever was being asked of them.

Some people have been asked to promise that a vendetta will be continued, or asked to promise they will save a family home from being foreclosed. Others have been asked to take care of a family member or take care of a friend's family, or to assume financial responsibility for someone. The list of unreasonable demands goes on and on of the different kinds of things people are asked to promise as the person is taking his last breath.

But is it fair to ask someone to stand in your stead after you are gone, to be responsible for the things that you didn't or couldn't do? And, as such, is it fair to expect someone to honor that deathbed promise, especially knowing that you have put him in such an unfair and untenable position?

CHAPTER 41
A GOOD LIAR

Are you a good liar? Can you recognize when a person is lying, and how reliable are the polygraphs, the tests to determine if someone is lying?

Someone who is not a practiced liar will probably show signs of nervousness or breaking out in a cold sweat when lying about something that is crucial. Their eyes could be dead giveaways or their body language could give many clues.

However, when it comes to a practiced liar or a pathological liar or a compulsive liar, the odds are that you won't be able to spot it.

142 • A SOUL'S GUIDE TO METAPHYSICS AND SPIRITUALITY

I have listened to pathological liars and they are so convincing that you would swear they are telling the truth. The first time I ever heard the term was more than fifty years ago. A woman was telling me that she was bilked out of $10,000 by a pathological liar ($10,000 in those days was a fortune, and it was this woman's entire life's savings).

I had no experience with pathological liars at the time, so I was not expecting this pretty face with the look of innocence about her. This was the same woman who had bilked the other one out of all that money so I knew not to let down my guard but she looked and sounded so honest that I would never have seen it coming if I hadn't been warned.

In later years, one of my clients had to take a polygraph test. She was a substance abuser and was applying for a job in a hospital where she would have access to prescription drugs. I asked her how she was going to pass the polygraph test and she smiled and told me she would pass it with flying colors. And she did. She got that hospital job and she was able to steal large amounts of narcotics.

Ten years later, another client was found to be a pathological liar. She could look you in the eye and tell you the most outrageous lie with the straightest face and you'd swear she was telling you the truth.

I'm in doubt that police departments, the FBI, the CIA, or any other law enforcement agency will ever have a reliable test to ascertain if someone is telling the truth. So, as of now, the only way I'd believe someone's story about a crime that was committed, is with DNA evidence.

CHAPTER 42
POSTING A BAD REVIEW? THINK AGAIN

This is one of those horror stories about customer feedback that is so hard to believe, yet it's true.

Whenever you buy something online, you get an email asking you to take a survey and to post your opinion of the product and the customer service you received.

You also have the option of posting your feedback online so that other customers can benefit from your experience. But wait a minute. Think again. Apparently, if you exercise that option, you and your credit rating can be ruined for all time.

I just read a news story about a couple who had bought some merchandise from a company and they didn't read the fine print of the contract. It seems that the terms of the service contained a clause that prohibited customers from posting negative reviews.

Since I am neither a friend nor relative of the couple, and since I didn't buy anything from KlearGear.com, nor did I sign any contract with them, I feel free to write my opinion of their unscrupulous business ethics, or lack of them, as the case may be.

The husband in this case, bought his wife some trinkets from this company. Thirty days elapsed, and they didn't send the merchandise. This led to the automatic canceling of PayPal's order.

His wife tried calling the company to find out what happened to her trinkets but she was never able to make contact with anyone. In sheer frustrstion, she took her complaint to the website, Ripoff Report saying that the company had "incompetent customer service" and "there is absolutely no way to get in touch with a physical human being."

To my way of thinking, that is a factual statement and contained no malice. KlearGear.com took exception to that and three years later, her husband received an email from KlearGear.com claiming he owed the company thousands of dollars as a result of the complaint on Ripoff Report for violating the terms of the contract and giving a negative review.

In the meantime, KlearGear.com ruined this couple's credit rating. Now they can't even get a loan to buy a car or fix the furnace in their home. They can't even afford to hire an attorney. The only recourse open to them is the one they took; they are now working with a separate credit company to try to have the mess cleared up.

CHAPTER 43
THE JUDGE DOES STAND-UP COMEDY

I've known a lot of judges in my day, both socially and as clients, but I can't say that any one of them struck me as being funny enough to do stand-up comedy.

Some of them had a sense of humor and had interesting cases that they talked about, but none of them were humorous enough to entertain an audience.

Now comes the story of a judge who, for the last ten years, has been doing precisely that. He's warmed up audiences for Comedy Central's "The Daily Show" and "The Colbert

148 · A SOUL'S GUIDE TO METAPHYSICS AND SPIRITUALITY

Report" and has performed at the Comedy Club on a regular basis. He performs about 250 gigs a year and is a member of the Screen Actors Guild.

On stage, he has made a name for himself for his edgy brand of humor and his targets have been children and the homophobic and racist characters that he has portrayed.

It's amazing that it has taken ten years for his moonlighting career to catch up with him. In a unanimous decision, the state Supreme Court told him that he must either give up his comedy work or step down from his position as a judge. Apparently, he prefers to make people laugh because he gave up his judicial position in favor of his comedy routine.

It was pointed out by a blogger that Justices of the Supreme Court, such as Sonia Sotomayor, have appeared on "The Colbert Report" and thus, "It's hard to say that a venue graced by a Supreme Court justice lacks the proper judicial dignity."

The difference here is that Justice Sonia Sotomayor was a guest on a comedy show; she wasn't doing stand-up comedy. This is much the same as various presidents appearing on comedy shows as guests but not doing stand-up comedy routines on those shows.

In another twist, the Assembly Minority Leader from the same state, also moonlights as a comedian. However, it seems hypocritical of him to say that the judge's comedy work undermines his standing on the court and not think that his own comedy work undermines his standing as the leader of his party.

There is one good thing about the former judge's decision to step down from the bench. He is still licensed to practice law in his state and, if his comedy career doesn't work out, he might win his court cases by making the jurors laugh.

CHAPTER 44
BANANA PEEL LAWSUIT LEADS TO ARREST

You would think that in this day and age, even the greediest and dumbest, would know that there are surveillance cameras on all kinds of public transportation.

Litigation has become such a spectator sport that government isn't taking any chances that people can sue them for fraudulent claims. Therefore, it is even funnier that a passenger thought he could get away with suing the Metro system for $15,000 on a phony claim that his hip and leg had been injured because of their negligence.

You can see on the surveillance video a man riding in an elevator. As the door opens, he makes himself look like he has slipped on something, lunging forward and to the ground.

What he doesn't realize is that the surveillance camera has caught him staring intently at the camera three times and then he throws a banana peel behind him so that he doesn't actually slip on anything; he just makes it look as though he slipped.

He complained that the custodian for the station had not cleaned up the floor prior to his entering the elevator, yet the camera footage shows that just prior to this man's boarding, there is nothing on the floor and the man is seen with what appears to be a banana peel in his hand, tossing it on the floor behind him. And all this time, he is seen looking in the direction of the camera.

How dumb can you be? If you know that you intend to commit a felony, you don't stand there in full view of a camera, staring at it intently, enough times to be identified for a mug shot. And you especially don't stand in front of a camera with the evidence (a banana peel) in your hand and throw it behind you if you intend to make it look as though you tripped on something that was already on the floor.

No, if you have every intention of defrauding the Metro system, you take several trips on it and look around carefully for where surveillance cameras are placed before coming back a final time to do your dirty deed, and you especially don't stare at the camera while you are committing the felony. Needless to say, he was arrested and charged with fraudulent injury claim.

CHAPTER 45
CHERISHED MEMORIES

This morning, I happened to glance at an ad for fuzzy winter bedroom slippers and immediately, across the tableau of my memories, was this vivid recollection of one of life's embarrassing moments. Keep in mind that I was very young at the time.

My boyfriend was traveling from a different direction and I was to meet him outside the train station so we could take the train into the city to do some shopping and see a play. In the old days, and living in a metropolitan area, men and women dressed very differently than they do today. Men wore suits, white shirts, and ties. Women wore girdles, stockings, and bras, although in those days bras and girdles were called foundations. Women also wore suits, high heels, hats, and gloves.

I mentioned that I was living in a metropolitan area at the time because there was a vast difference between the metropolitan dress code and the dress code that one would encounter in the suburbs. In the city, you couldn't even get into a restaurant without being suitably attired.

I remember a story about Carol Channing, the famous actress, going into a restaurant in a pair of slacks. The maitre d' stopped her at the door and told her that she couldn't be seated if she was wearing slacks. She told him she would be right back. She went out to her car and retrieved her mink coat and walked back into the restaurant wearing her mink coat over her slacks. She was seated immediately.

I wasn't Carol Channing and I didn't have a mink coat in the back of my car so I had to dress according to our very formal dress code if I wanted to be admitted into the theater and into a restaurant after the play. Because this date with my boyfriend was for a very special occasion, my mother allowed me to borrow one of her chic, dressy suits. I was going to wear my own leather gloves, hat, heels, and leather purse. When I left the house, I felt good about my appearance. I knew I was dressed in the height of fashion.

I was about a block away from the train station and I could see my boyfriend doubled over and he was pointing and laughing. I looked around and couldn't see anything that would cause him to laugh so uncontrollably. When I reached him, he could barely talk for laughing so hard and all he could do was point down at my feet.

My face turned a bright red. There I was, dressed to the nines, feeling great about going into the city like an adult, and I was wearing my pink, fuzzy, bunny slippers with this sophisticated outfit.

CHAPTER 46
LIVING IN A DISPOSABLE WORLD

Sometimes it seems as though we are living in a disposable world. We've gone from disposable tissues, to disposable diapers, to disposable spouses, to disposable income. It's almost as though we are holding someone's place, waiting for them to fill it after we're through with it.

Most couples who marry young go through a growth spurt and they often outgrow their partner. Their interests change and, consequently, their needs also change. If they are in the same career or the same business, it's possible they can grow together but, more often than not, they drift apart until, suddenly, one of them feels the need to change the status quo.

Transitions can be scary but they can also be great opportunities. It can be a wonderful adventure where you feel as though you are starting with a blank canvas and you can fill it with anything that catches your interest. On the other hand, if you let yourself slide into fear, it can be a nightmare.

It's so easy to get into a rut. Fear can do that. You can feel a physical and emotional paralysis and not have the energy to think beyond your crisis. But if you force yourself to take small steps each day, it might not be necessary for life to throw you in at the deep end in a sink or swim crisis.

Divorce or widowhood doesn't have to be the end of the world. It could open doors that you never knew were shut. You could discover hidden talents that would never have come to light if you had stayed married.

I'm not suggesting that everyone gets divorced just to discover their hidden talents and opportunities for growth. However, I am saying that if it happens, don't be afraid of it. You may discover that if you had stayed married, you'd never have tried to develop those talents.

Maybe with people living longer these days, we're meant to be place holders for other people and they're meant to be place holders for us. Maybe we're all just part of this disposable society for our own growth and development and maybe we're part of this disposable society for the growth and development of others. I have a feeling that someday, before the end of our life, we'll find the answers.

CHAPTER 47
CHOOSING YOUR BATTLES CAREFULLY

When I was much younger, everything seemed so important and I argued passionately for so many issues. And then I got older and realized that most things are relatively unimportant.

If you're married or living with a roommate, who cares if the towels are folded this way or that way? In the larger scheme of things, who cares how the dishwasher is stacked or if the dishes are left in the sink? If your spouse were to suddenly die or become disabled, will these issues still seem important?

I have always argued to the death for my principles and that will never change. Don't ask me to violate my principles, not while I still have breath to argue for them and to try to do everything to defend them. But anything else? Not likely.

There is one other thing that is important enough for me to argue about. If you and I were married and you weren't a fiscally responsible person, I wouldn't allow my name to be on any legal documents that we shared. That means no bank loans, no house mortgage, no credit cards and, definitely, no joint bank accounts. In fact, I would do my banking in a different bank so that you would never have access to my accounts.

If you want to buy a house and I don't, you can buy it in your name and not put my name on the deed. You would be responsible for the mortgage payments and I would share utility bills and grocery bills, not much of anything else. Same thing if the reverse were true. If I wanted to buy a house and you didn't, the house would be in my name and I'd be responsible for the mortgage payments and the maintenance costs, and we would share the utility bills and groceries.

Couples often have different spending habits and core values. If you want to spend your money on what I call stupid things, that's your prerogative, but don't spend my money on those things. We'd have separate bank accounts and you can spend your money on anything you want; just don't touch my money or ask me to spend my money on things that I don't want.

Government is always spending my money on things that are not essential and that I don't want but, other than trying to vote those legislators out of office, there isn't much I can do about that.

Through the years, I have come to realize that most of the things that cause us unhappiness today, will not even be in our lives five or ten years from now. We will barely even remember them five or ten years from now so, nowadays, whenever something upsets me, I ask myself if this issue will still be important to me five or ten years from now, and if it won't, I make myself drop it and put my focus elsewhere.

Many of my clients have been with me thirty or forty years, so I have the benefit of having shared their fears and tears and, when they have different issues now, that are causing them extreme distress, I remind them about a person or about a situation from all those years ago. Most of them do remember the situation that I'm referring to but when I ask them if those people are important to them now, or if they are still stressing out over the same situation, so far, no one has said yes.

If those people and/or situations are not still in our lives five or ten years after the fact, how important could they have been? As long as we have free will, we can change the outcome of the various scenarios by using our creativity and whatever resources are at our disposal. As children, we don't have many options to extricate ourselves from painful situations but, as adults, we do.

We can only control just so much in our lives and no more. We can make healthy eating choices and exercise. We can meditate and not allow ourselves to be in toxic relationships. We can do everything within our power to eliminate the stress in our lives but we cannot control the world around us. The only thing we can control is ourselves and how we respond to the world around us.

Nowadays, when faced with an unpleasant situation that I can't control and can't do anything about, instead of getting angry, I ask myself if this argument is worth dying on the hill for. Time and distance have shown me that most of the time, the arguments that you thought were so important are not worth dying on the hill for.

CHAPTER 48
AFTER YOUR GIFT HAS BEEN DELIVERED

There has been so much in the news about the advances made in robotic science, that it gives one pause to question whether one should hold onto old emotional prejudices.

We see robots being taught to do complex things like solving Rubik's Cube in a matter of seconds. We see them being taught to use their powers of observation to make emotional decisions. It is no longer a matter of watching a robot vacuuming your house or bringing you a drink or turning on your oven to start your dinner before you get home from work. Now, they are being taught to think and to build other robots just like themselves.

About six months ago, we saw a clip of a car driving itself down the Autobahn, the most dangerous 8,000 mile network in Germany where the human driver of the car climbed over the back seat to test the robotic safety system of the Infiniti Q50 to see how active the Active Lane Control feature really is, but there was no clip to show us that this robotic feature had any emotions while taking over the functions of a human driver.

I was just about getting ready to set aside my human panic attack at seeing some of these daredevil stunts done by robots when a very human thought occurred to me.

This had nothing to do with the kinds of extraordinary things that today's robots are being taught. One of those things that robots are being taught is to sit in front of a TV and watch the way humans act, how they emote, how they interact with other humans, etc. In fact, they are being taught, by watching TV, how to think and how to behave just like us.

No, this thought that roams around in my head has nothing to do with that. It has to do with the human emotion of gift giving. When you don't live near enough to your friend or relative to give him or her a birthday present or a Christmas present, the best you can do is talk to each other on the phone or see each other on Skype. But that doesn't really do it for most of us.

There's no robot that can tap into my excitement when a family member sends me an unusual gift. We have a tradition of opening our gifts by phone.

When my birthday rolls around, I don't want to look at the clock and see that it's after midnight, so it's all right to open my gifts because it's legitimately my birthday. No, I want to open my gift with my family member on the other end of the phone so that our real reactions to the gift comes through the wires. A robot will never be able to take the place of someone I love.

And, if I send a gift, do I really want a robot to thank me for it? No, I do not. If I send someone flowers, I want to hear the person's voice on the other end of the phone telling me what the flowers look like and if they have a nice fragrance or whether the arrangement looks like the picture of it that I saw online.

I don't want a robot thanking me for the flowers I sent; I want to share the emotions that went with selecting the gift for someone special. I want to feel that excitement, and no robot can replace that emotion for me.

CHAPTER 49
IS IT REALLY BETTER TO GIVE THAN TO RECEIVE?

We have all heard the bible verse that it is better to give than to receive but that may not necessarily be the case. In fact, this may be at the root of the breakdown of a relationship.

More relationships have been ruined because one does all the giving and the other one does all the taking. In other words, it's not a balanced relationship and this often causes resentment in both partners.

168 • A SOUL'S GUIDE TO METAPHYSICS AND SPIRITUALITY

This is one of the ways it could play out: A couple may start out with the understanding that since they both go to work, it's only fair that they divide the household chores equally between them. The wife may take the cooking and the husband may take the laundry and for several months, this division of labor is working very well.

One day, the wife gets home from work early and she finishes the cooking in record time and then she decides to surprise her husband by doing his chore, the laundry. When he comes home and discovers that his wife has done the laundry and he has clean clothing, he is ecstatic. He thanks his wife exuberantly and they are both in a great mood that night.

This goes on for a while. The wife has been getting off early each week and when she finishes her cooking she does his laundry. However, as the weeks go by, his enthusiasm seems to diminish and by the time a month has passed, he's barely acknowledging that she has been doing his chore and her own.

Then, one day the wife is very busy at work and when she gets home she barely has time to get dinner on the table. After dinner, the husband goes looking for a clean shirt and sees that all of his shirts are in the dirty laundry. He's really angry because he has to go somewhere that evening and he has nothing to wear.

"Where are my shirts," he asks. "They must be in the laundry," answers his wife. "Why didn't you do the laundry?" he asks in a very demanding tone of voice, "Now I don't have a clean shirt for tonight." Instead of the wife telling him that the laundry is his job, she starts to make all kinds of excuses for why she didn't do it.

No one likes to be taken for granted. When you show appreciation, most people will bend over backward to please you. But there is also an underlying lesson to be learned and that is when you do too much it becomes expected and, then when you stop doing, the other person gets angry and can't understand why you are no longer giving as much as you used to. And this can very often be the beginning of the breakdown of a relationship because the giving and the receiving need to be balanced.

CHAPTER 50

WHY DON'T PEOPLE GRIEVE ALIKE?

I used to wonder why people didn't grieve alike. I would go to funerals and see some people trying to throw themselves into the ground with their loved one in a casket. Others stood there stoically, not shedding a tear, some mourners stood silently, letting tears stream down their faces but not uttering a sound, and others cried so loud you could hear them in the next county.

It wasn't until I got older and had been to a lot of funerals and shared a lot of stories with my clients, that I began to ascertain the answers to my question. And, the answer is so simple that I'm almost embarrassed I didn't see it when I was fourteen and fifteen and trying to figure it out, but in those days, people didn't discuss these things, especially with children.

As I got older and experienced more of life, and let me qualify that. As I got older and more of my loved ones died, I began to understand the answers without my elders saying a word to me. They didn't have to say a word; the answers were written on the faces of the mourners.

How people express grief depends on their emotional experiences. Some people have been made to feel they are weak and inferior if they show any outward signs of grief. Others want to be seen as loving the deceased one so thoroughly that they can't contain their emotions. And others can't cry in public.

I'm one of those people who can't cry in public. I usually take my grief and suffer silently, in my bedroom, or just away from other people. On rare occasions, when my body can't contain the emotions that are clamoring for release, I might stand there silently and not even realize that the tears are flowing down my face. But. shortly afterward, I hie myself off to a private place to grieve by myself.

So now, many generations later, when I hear people criticizing mourners who don't shed a tear, those who stand silently as though this was just another day, another occasion, another funeral, I look at the faces of the people who are there and I'm more cognizant of pain-filled eyes and smiles for their guests that don't reach their eyes, and I realize that they are grieving in their own way, and it's not for any of us to stand in judgment of how the death of a loved one has affected them.

We're different people, shaped by different experiences, and we're dealing with grief in the only way we know how.

CHAPTER 51

WHY DO PEOPLE DISAPPOINT US?

The better question would be, why do we expect so much from our family and friends that we leave ourselves open to disappointment?

In times of trouble, most people go to their family or friends for emotional support some, even, for financial support. But, do we have the right to expect them to drop everything and help us through our crises?

It usually depends on the type of relationships that are in place. On a good day, we can acknowledge that the other person has his or her own life and his or her own problems. On a bad day, we may not be that understanding. It's on those bad days that we may feel that we have given so much and received so little in return, and many relationships fall by the wayside after the crisis has passed and the person is left licking his wounds and feeling like the relationship has been one-sided.

What do we put into our relationships and what should we expect in return? In most relationships, one person usually gives more than the other but, in a good relationship, when the giver needs the support of the other, it's usually forthcoming.

Not everyone is good at talking about his problems and asking for help. In that case, are you expecting your friend or family member to be a mind reader, to know what you are thinking and feeling? Shouldn't they know instinctively when all is not right in your world and offer to help you?

The answer is that your expectations may be slightly skewed because you're expecting them to be mind readers and most people are not mind readers. Most people cannot tune into your mind and figure out what's going on with you unless you tell them. And, if you're not good at communicating, you may be left feeling that no one cares about you and you can't go to anyone for help.

Then, there is the opposite of that. You may have to ask yourself if you've gone to them for help too often and taken advantage of their friendship. It's a delicate balance. Sometimes we have to give more than we get, but over the long haul, things either have to balance out or we have to look for someone else to take their place.

CHAPTER 52

INSTANT TRUST, INSTANT BETRAYAL

We do so many things that are geared to instant everything. We want instant gratification, instant attraction, instant relationships, and, yes, we even want instant hookups and instant sex. In short, we want everything to happen immediately and we want the best possible outcomes.

Is this possible? I suppose that anything is possible but is it realistic? Probably not.

People used to take a long time between the first meeting and marriage; nowadays, shortly after the first meeting, they are picking out china patterns and looking at houses. Somehow or other, they are bypassing the romantic interlude of getting to know each other very well before committing to a lifetime of wedded bliss.

A woman was talking about a man she had known for three months. They dated casually but nothing was said about the future and, when he stopped seeing her because he was moving back to his own country, she felt betrayed. Her words, "I trusted him and now I feel betrayed."

How could you trust someone you've only known three months? Trust is something that doesn't happen overnight. It takes a long time to develop and that's only after going through endless experiences and the other person has been proven to be trustworthy. How can you feel betrayed after such a short time of knowing each other?

We often hear about couples who have been married for twenty-five or thirty years where one of the spouses cleans out the bank account of the other spouse and runs off with all their material possessions. And that's with knowing each other for over two decades and building up a level of trust all those years.

If the spouse who was left with nothing complains about having trusted the other one and been betrayed, that would be a valid complaint. But trusting someone after just three months of casual dating and feeling betrayed for going back to his own country? That's not only unrealistic, it also feels delusional, or at the very least, like FantasyLand.

If people who have known and trusted each other for decades can betray each other, it stands to reason that trust should not be given lightly. In matters of the heart and material possessions, instant trust seems both foolish and ill-considered.

CHAPTER 53

HAVING IT ALL

I just ran across an interesting article about how men and women define having it all and I have to say that I disagree with their conclusion.

First of all, their survey is confined to professionals and, second of all, they only surveyed 1,000 people. A survey of only 1,000 people isn't very much of a survey and it didn't say whether it was taken nationwide, cross-country, or if it was confined to one part of the country.

If the survey was taken in the south, the answers might be very different from the views of the people in the north, or the east from the west. And if it was a cross-section of people, that would only give them 250 people in each part of the country, not a very impressive number.

Perhaps if their survey's premise was that their concept of having it all in terms of career, money, marriage, and children, was confined to professionals, the article might not have caught my eye. However, there was nothing in their conclusion that broke down their numbers, not their ages, careers, religions, races, socioeconomic groups, or geographical locations.

That said, their conclusion is "79 percent of guys think a strong, loving marriage plays a part in having it all, whereas only 66 percent of ladies say the same. In fact, not only do fewer women than men feel that marriage is key, but the number of women who say that neither marriage nor relationships factor into their definition has nearly doubled over the past year: from five percent in 2012 to nine percent in 2013.

"And when it comes to kids, 86 percent of dudes consider them part of their "having it all" definition - but for women, that number's only 73 percent."

My clients come from every part of the world and they span all religions, socioeconomic groups, and all ages, and their answers to that survey are vastly different.

There are very few women, single, divorced, career-oriented, or stay at home personalities, who don't want to be in a committed relationship. In fact, the thing I hear most often is, "Am I destined to be alone? When am I going to meet my soul mate? Am I ever going to meet someone with whom I can have a committed relationship?

And most of them are looking for family. They want to have children and they want to "have it all."

CHAPTER 54
WHAT FAIRY TALES TAUGHT US

Most of us grew up on fairy tales and we went on to reading them to other kids, those we babysat for and those we parented. Most of us took something from those stories and let them influence our lives in subtle ways.

The story of Cinderella is a classic example. Little girls listened to the words being read to them and in their subconscious mind they waited for Prince Charming to sweep them off their feet and carry them off into the sunset, knowing that they would never have to worry about anything because their prince would take care of everything.

Snow White is another one. In one version of the story, Snow White falls into a poison-induced sleep until her prince wakes her up with a kiss. Writers often use the imagery to suggest that a woman who is experiencing lovemaking for the first time, has been asleep all her life and she is now awakened.

Then, there is the tale of Rapunzel who is being held a prisoner in a tower by an enchantress. She is very beautiful and the enchantress wants her kept away from the world so she puts her in a tower that has no doors. Every day, she would call up to Rapunzel to let down her hair so that she can climb up to see her.

One day, the king's son sees her and falls in love with her but he doesn't see a way of getting to her. The next day, he hears the enchantress telling Rapunzel to let down her hair so that she can climb her golden stair. The next night, the prince calls up to her to let down her hair so that he can help her escape.

And, once again, little girls who heard this story, took with them the thought that their prince would come to their aid and all their problems would be solved.

We have gone through generations of girls wanting to be princesses, taken care of by a prince, and boys being taught that they had to protect girls and take care of them.

Fairy tales wouldn't be fairy tales if there was a healthy dose of realism in those stories, but it sure would have led a lot of women to chart their own destiny instead of waiting for a man to take care of all their needs.

CHAPTER 55

IS IT KINDNESS OR COWARDICE?

I have watched people being emotionally abused try to justify their inaction. When asked why they allow it, they will say something like, "I'm just too kind."

Wrong. They are not being too kind; they are being cowardly. They lack the courage to handle confrontation. They shrivel up inside at the thought of conflict and run away from any sort of argument. These are the people who will roll over and play dead and let you rob them of their possessions and their dignity.

There are people who think that if you have an argument it means the relationship is over. The next step is going to an attorney and filing for a divorce; they don't stop to think that an argument can clear the air and help you to see each other's point of view. It doesn't occur to them that after the unpleasantness passes, your relationship can be so much better.

If I had to differentiate between kindness and cowardice it would be that with cowardice you don't want to let someone abuse you or take your possessions but you allow it to happen without saying anything.

Kindness, on the other hand, has you offering whatever you have to others without thinking of the cost or the hardship. It's giving with an open hand and an open heart. It's giving of yourself because that's your nature and you feel good about whatever it is you are giving.

When clients are so self-absorbed that they can't see beyond themselves, I have them volunteer in soup kitchens on holidays or work with the homeless. I've been known to tell them to get in touch with Big Brother Big Sister and spend time with a child who is having a difficult time. I also have them do volunteer work in hospitals and old age homes. And little by little they open their hearts to connect with humanity.

People who have a generosity of spirit are unique. They are the ones who reach out to those in need without being asked to do so. They have an innate kindness that allows them to give unstintingly but they also have boundaries that keep you from taking advantage of them.

It feels so much nicer to accept help from someone who gives it to you out of kindness than one who allows you to take it out of cowardice.

CHAPTER 56

MY SPIRITUAL PLAYGROUND

Don't gasp. The title of this article isn't heresy or blasphemous; it's just a memoir of my early days of committing myself to the spiritual path.

I was thinking of those early days when I had no one to guide me and I relied heavily on those assorted books that raised more questions than answered them.

The very first book that I read should have sent me running in the opposite direction but my innate curiosity won out and I started my first investigation. The book centered on the dangers of the kundalini energy and how you can become insane if those energies are misdirected. The author went into graphic detail about how he went insane from it. For a very long time, I forced myself to stay away from it. When I finally experienced it, the feeling was so exquisite that I had a hard time putting a description into words. The closest I could come was the vision of bright midday sun in a midnight sky with billions of stars surrounding it. The kundalini lasted three weeks and then disappeared. It was the most glorious feeling of peace and energy combined and as much as I miss it, I feel very blessed for having experienced it for those three weeks.

I should also mention that I was so determined to open my channel and put my chakras into balance that I meditated seven to eight hours a day every day for several years. When the rest of the world was asleep, I was meditating.

Those first several years were like magic. I tried everything. I would read a book and get some ideas about what I could try next. It never occurred to me that I would run up against something I couldn't do so I succeeded at everything I tried.

One day, I was packing my bags to go on a business trip and a thought came into my mind. I grinned to myself and I thought, "why not?" It was a visualization out of left field and something that would never have occurred to me. I sat for a few minutes and focused intently. I visualized a gorgeous man sitting next to me on the plane, neither of us saying a word and me writing a poem, still not speaking. Just as the plane was boarding, the most gorgeous man, movie-star gorgeous, put his briefcase in the overhead compartment, looked down at me and nodded, and sat down next to me, neither of us saying a word. Just as we were landing, I finished my poem and we each departed without saying a word. "Holy Moley," I thought. "This is the first time this has ever happened. Usually, when I'm on a plane, or actually, wherever I go, people are always talking to me, telling me their life stories." It was such a refreshing change to be able to sit in silence, thinking my own thoughts without having to listen or make conversation with someone I'll never see again. This man filled my visualization perfectly. He was gorgeous, didn't speak to me, didn't try to see what I was writing, and left the plane without a word being spoken. And, I got a chance to write a poem which I then included in a book I was writing.

I think visualizations are the loveliest things in my spiritual toybox and I used to employ them every chance I got. Keep in mind that this was when I first got into metaphysics; nowadays, I reserve them for important things...but this was then, not now.

In the old days, when your car was towed, they sent

someone to your house to drive you back to their shop where you would pay your bill, and then you would drive their driver back to their shop. This was one of those days. As I was driving the towing car driver back to her shop I looked up and saw a big rain cloud in the distance and said, "It looks like it's going to rain." In a snarly voice, she said, "It's already raining and we're going to get soaked." I didn't like her tone of voice and as intently as I could, I visualized the rain going everywhere but not a drop hitting my car so I said, "The cars on the left will get wet. The cars on the right will get wet. The cars behind me and in front of me will get wet but this car that I'm driving will not get wet. The rain will not touch it." As I was driving along, I noticed all the cars getting wet but I didn't hear a drop of rain hitting any part of my car. When we got back to the shop, I turned to her and said, "See? There isn't a drop of rain on my car; it's completely dry." She took one look at me and ran off as if the hounds of hell were after her.

While I was driving home, I noticed that my car was still dry even though it was still pouring. As soon as I got into my house and closed the door behind me, the rain came down in buckets but I was still dry. That night, around 3:00 a.m., I decided to walk over to the dumpster to dump my garbage because the rain had stopped. As I was walking across the grass the lawn sprinklers came on, full force, spraying upwards, drenching my suit and shoes. It dawned on me then that I had visualized the rain that was coming down had stopped, but I had forgotten to visualize the sprinklers on the ground being in the off position. I hope God got a good laugh out of that one.

I had such a good time finding out that I could manifest whatever I thought of that I didn't consider the possibility that there are some things that I should never attempt.

One day, I was thinking about someone and all of a sudden, my eyes focused on a sentence in a book that I was reading. It said that you should never use your powers to influence another person's actions or thought of visualizing a person doing something or giving me something that I wanted. It simply had never occurred to me that I could get someone to do what I wanted just by visualizing it. But now there was a spiritual commandment that said there would be heavy negative karma attached to it if I used the power of visualization that way. I mulled it over and knew that this was something that felt like an intrusion on someone's life so it wouldn't be something that I would want to try. Later in the day, I tried to find that passage in the book I had been reading and I couldn't find it. I searched every page and still couldn't find it.

This kind of thing has always happened to me. From

time to time. whenever something is very important, a bright yellow message would appear on a page I was reading. It has always felt like a call to action or a warning to stop me from doing something I was doing or planning to do. The first few times this happened, I tried to tell people about it but they wouldn't believe me. One of my biggest arguments came when I told my friend that Ford had pardoned Nixon and she said that he hadn't and I argued that he had. A week later, the news came out that Nixon had been pardoned. But I had seen that newspaper article in print the week before although it had been in a bright yellow font. This may have been the beginning of my awareness that a higher power was at work and never to question it.

Never to question it? I had always questioned everything. How could I not question everything? This was a very steep learning curve for me. Sometimes I would get a message or a feeling that a piece of information was for me so that I would get an accurate picture of something but I wasn't allowed to share that information. This was, and still is after all these years, very difficult for me to do because I have always shared information with those who needed it. Nonetheless, when I get that message, I always heed it because I know that there is a higher power at work and I will be stopped from uttering those words.

My first experience came with a client. I saw so clearly what was happening and tried to tell her to change course. However, every time I started to tell her what I was seeing, different words came out of my mouth. As soon as she left and I heard her car drive away, I remembered everything I had wanted to say. In the end, it was a good thing she didn't change course because she had a great deal of negative karma from her past relationship with this man and if she had changed course, she wouldn't have been able to fulfill her negative karma with him. By staying the course, she was forced to change the behavior pattern that eventually led her into a much better relationship with a different man a few years later.

In the beginning, everything was so new and shiny that the years were filled with joy and excitement. My body could scarcely contain all the excitement and wonder that I was feeling. I learned about sending divine love and light to people and that we are the microcosm of the macrocosm and man being the microcosm and that divine spark that lives within each of us is a replica of perfection.

With that in mind, every time I would see someone, I would mentally send him or her divine love and light. I had been doing this for quite some time when I finally told my friend what I was doing. She chastised me for doing it to everyone I saw; she thought it should only be done for people who really needed it. I stopped doing it for a short while so I could think about it and meditate on it. In the end, I went back to it because I thought everyone needed God's love and light and by directing it to the divine spark in everyone, I was lifting the vibration of the planet up a notch. Now, more than ever, people need to spread love and light to everyone because we are more in need of spiritual guidance than ever before. Also, do not mix up the distinction between God's love and romantic love and lust; they are poles apart.

God accepts us as we are; His love is infinite and unconditional while human love is filled with conditions and expectations. Even when we've looked forward to getting something and we can't get what we want and we put a good face on it, there is still the tinge of disappointment that we feel. I think since God is omniscient He knew at the time He created the universe that man will err and commit nefarious deeds but He will still love us with all our human foibles. And maybe we commit offenses against humanity with more ease than we should because we know in our hearts that God will still love us and forgive us.

I used to wonder if God still loved Hitler after all the

horrific crimes he committed against humanity but then one day I concluded that He could still love the divine spark of perfection that He created within Hitler. I'll never know if my theory is accurate but it comforts me to know that no amount of retributive karma could eradicate the negative karma that Hitler deserves to reap for sending millions of people to the gas chambers among other things. Whenever I think of God forgiving Hitler for all his atrocities, I have to remind myself that God's love is a spiritual love and that's the part of Hitler that God can still love and forgive. Since I'm not at that level of evolvement, I reserve the right to want to see him punished for every person who suffered at his hands in exactly the same way he caused their suffering.

I still wonder if we will ever get to the point where all souls will have reached the level of God Consciousness at the same time, each soul having attained it individually but gathering together as one, in peace, love, and harmony. Will we be able to communicate with each other telepathically, with just our thoughts or emotions, but no words, or will we still need words? The one thing that has always plagued me is how words often get misinterpreted or misunderstood and often leave people with unresolved anger or disappointment. We often come close to this level of communication when we use our intuition but that doesn't happen often enough to help people over the rough spots. I think I see it most often when one person suspects his or her partner of infidelity. Then it comes into play in a brutal way. We saw this happening when Princess Diana suspected Prince Charles of having an affair while still on their honeymoon. The rest of their marriage was a crash and burn scenario, ending with the death of Princess Diana. There is still the specter hanging over their heads as to whether it was an automobile collision and a real accident or whether it was a planned murder. There is enough evidence on both sides to support both theories.

While most marriages do not end up with that kind of violence, it stands to reason that telepathy might have been very useful at the beginning of their courtship. If Diana had suspected Charles of still being in love with Camila, she might not have married him and she still could have reaped her karma with him in a different way.

The subject of metaphysics is a very deep one and I suspect none of us will be able to do more than scratch the surface and still walk away only understanding a fraction of it. I doubt if atheists and various religious leaders will ever agree on the meaning of various biblical events and there will always be wars reminiscent of The Crusades.

As I said before, we need God's love and guidance more now than at any other time of our lives. Let's join our hands and hearts and focus on a world at peace, with understanding, tolerance, and love uniting us all in spiritual harmony and love.

CHAPTER 57

MY SPIRITUAL TOY BOX

I never played with toys so I never had a toy box but once I got into metaphysics I found the most wondrous toys in the world. I discovered things I could only dream about if I had known about them. But, never too late. I have them now and I'm holding on tightly to them because it might be dangerous if you don't know how to use them wisely.

Visualization is one of my favorite toys. If I really want something, all I have to do is visualize it completely and then put the force of my will behind it, and lo and behold, I can manifest it. As I said, this can be very dangerous if you don't know how to use it wisely.

First of all, you don't use it on people. You don't try to manipulate them by visualizing something that will affect them adversely. You can visualize them getting well but not getting sick. The negative karma attached to such an action is overwhelming. So, if you have a bone to pick with someone, do it in the traditional way; have a discussion.

My first visualization toy was looking for a white cloud that had a tiny black rain spot in it. My aim was to make the black spot disappear so that the cloud was completely white. This took a lot of practice. First, I had to find a completely white cloud with a tiny black rain spot in it. Then I had to make the black rain spot disappear so that the cloud could become completely white. My biggest challenge was finding a completely white cloud, then finding one with a tiny black rain spot in it. After I did it the first time, I kept practicing it so that I could do it all the time without having to think about it.

My next toy from my spiritual toy box was to see if I could see colors with my eyes closed and only a few fingers on a color. I thought this was going to be hard because the pages with the colors were on the other side of the paper. It turned out to be easier than I thought it would be. I sat with my eyes closed feeling each color. The first color I touched felt cool so

I said it was blue. When I opened my eyes I saw that the color really was blue. Then I closed my eyes again and shuffled the pages and touched another page and said that this page felt hot so I said it was red, and when I opened my eyes and looked at the paper, the color really was red. I did that with all the colors until I could identify all of them.

The fingers have memory cells. If you practice something over and over again, your fingers will automatically find the right place. It's kind of like practicing the piano. If you are trying to learn a very fast passage you may find it easier to take a small piece of it and play it slowly at first and as you play it over and over, each time increasing the speed until your fingers fly over the keys, you will be able to do it well enough to go on to the next section of the passage; it's no different with colors. Each time you touch a color, make sure that you identified the right color and, then practice running your fingers across it. Be aware of the heat or coolness of the color as well as the texture of it. Yes, there is a texture to colors as well as a vibratory force of each one and as you keep practicing it, you'll be able to feel the difference in each one.

In the very early days, I used to go to men's clothing stores and touch the ties. They used to have a wide variety of colored ties and I learned the difference in the feel of them. After I was proficient at that, I went on to learn the colors of slacks, suits, and shirts, all by touch until I could buy a shirt, and three weeks later, the color was in my mind and fingers and I could buy a tie that matched the shirt perfectly without having seen it all those weeks later.

There is no magic to this; it just requires intense concentration, focus, determination, practice, and perseverance. It also requires lots of patience.

As I was writing this, I thought of the words of the famous Indian guru, Paramahansa Yogananda, in his book, "Autobiography of a Yogi," he said that performing miracles is a matter of rearranging atoms and molecules. As soon as I read those words, I decided that I was going to try to rearrange the atoms and molecules of every task that seemed impossible. For the most part, I succeeded and the rare times I didn't succeed it was God's way of protecting me.

There is an old saying, "Be careful what you wish for because you will probably get it." If you do the visualization correctly and if your higher-self detects no danger will come to you, chances are that you will get your wish, It really is a case of rearranging the atoms and molecules and, once, again, I stress that you need to be careful about what you wish for and how you go about making it happen.

Many years ago, I was teaching someone the art of visualization. I told him to visualize what he wanted in its entirety. We had gone to Disneyland and we were deciding where we wanted to eat dinner. We didn't tell each other what we were visualizing and we agreed to meet at 5:00 p.m. and compare notes.

At 5:00 p.m. we met at the designated place and he was very dejected. It seems as though he told the maître d' that he was making dinner reservations for two and he was just going to get his friend. When he got back to the restaurant, his reservation had been canceled and we couldn't get in. I asked him to tell me how he visualized it and he told me that he made dinner reservations for two and he told the maître d' he was just going to get his friend but when he got back, his reservation had been canceled.

Then he asked me what I had visualized and I told him that I visualized going to a different restaurant that had fish tanks along all the walls with beautiful fish in them and that I visualized the two of us sitting at a table directly in front of them. I told him that I visualized us eating lobsters with wonderful French rolls and that we were smiling as we paid the bill for our delicious dinner. Then we went over to the restaurant and we were horrified to see a very long line that stretched as far as I could see it.

Still, optimist that I am, I went to the front of the line and asked the man who was taking reservations if we could get a table for two in front of the fish tanks. The man looked into the restaurant and said that a table was just being cleaned and we could be seated in a few minutes. True to his word, the table was cleaned within a few minutes and we were seated immediately in front of these beautiful fish tanks. Our lobsters and French rolls were delicious and we had smiles on our faces as we were paying our bill for our fabulous dinner.

After we left the restaurant, I sat the man down and told him why his visualization didn't work and why mine did work. I told him that the first part of his visualization was complete where he saw his reservation in the book in front of the fish tanks but the rest of his visualization was not complete. Instead of seeing us sitting at a table in front of the fish tanks eating a delicious dinner smiling as we were paying the bill, indicating that we had enjoyed our dinner, he left that part out, stopping at the point where he saw his name in the book for a table for two in front of the fish tanks and then leaving the restaurant to get me. My visualization was complete and that's why we were able to get a table immediately and leapfrogged over all those other people who were waiting in line for tables.

I usually tell people that the universe is like a five-year-old child. It understands simple directions. Don't confuse it with a lot of details and remember that your desire needs to be specific with details that are plain enough to be understood by a small child with limited communication skills and not enough experience to understand all the nuances of adult conversation. Just recently, I had an hour's consultation with a seven-year-old child and I treated it as if I were talking to the universe with very clear and very simple directions. Then, I spoke to the mother and made sure we were all on the same page by telling her exactly what I told her son, with his permission.

While the universe can't tell me in words that it understands what I want, a seven-year-old child can certainly tell me if I succeeded in reaching him. If I don't get what I'm asking for, I know that it's either that I confused the universe with my directions or God is protecting me by denying me what I'm asking for. When you boil it down to those two things it's very easy to see whether you will get what you want or not. If it's not a matter of God needing to protect you, then it's a matter of you not making your request clearly enough.

I made a lot of experiments with these spiritual toys. Every time I read a book that discussed one of them, I rushed home to try it out. One of these books talked about sending messages telepathically. That interested me greatly because I had once read that if we have a very strong emotion about something it can be picked up by someone fifty miles away. It said that if you are standing somewhere and someone angers you and you're feeling as though you could kill him, someone fifty miles away can pick up that thought and that emotion and he could pull out a knife or a gun and kill someone because he can feel the depth of your emotions and your thought and is acting on it.

With that in mind, I called my friend who lived fifty miles away and asked her to test this theory with me. Since we lived in different counties, I didn't have to worry that my answers would be based on her facial expressions or body movements. I told her to pick up ten items and concentrate very hard on each one individually, then, one by one I would tell her what she was holding, I got all ten right so I knew I could receive messages telepathically. Then, I tested her to see if she could receive my messages telepathically and she received them all accurately.

So now we knew. We could each send and receive messages telepathically. This now placed a burden on both of us. No longer could we assume that our thoughts and emotions affected no one but ourselves. We now had proof that everything we think and feel is being felt by someone else and is being processed accurately.

Shortly after that experiment, I picked up a book by Annie Besant called "Thought Forms" and found the most interesting thing to put in my spiritual toy box. It very clearly showed a physical description of your thoughts and emotions. It also showed your level of spirituality and your level of intelligence. If you are very spiritual, your aura will be clear and luminescent. If you are a nasty person or a jealous person, your aura or your thought forms will be dark and muddy. The book showed the colors and appearance of your thoughts and emotions and anyone who is psychic can see them, but those people who are not psychic and cannot see them can certainly feel them. So, now I knew. Whenever I met someone I didn't like it was because he or she had muddy thought forms and those I did like were because he or she had clear and beautiful thought forms and those thought forms can be felt and seen by everyone.

Since these were the early days of my entrance into metaphysics I didn't know anyone who could guide me so, left to my own devices, I tried everything. One day, one of the women I met took me aside and said, "You don't know Sabrina (not her real name) very well, so let me give you a warning. She is very jealous of you so watch your back and be very cautious around her."

I had a difficult time believing that anyone could be jealous of me but I heeded this woman's words anyway. One night, Sabrina rang my doorbell and she had a few friends and a crystal ball with her. To say I was astounded is putting it mildly. She introduced me to everyone and then she took out her crystal ball and said," We will each look into this crystal ball and tell everyone what we see. I'll go first." Then she took the crystal ball and started telling everyone what she was seeing. With a very self-satisfied smile, she handed the crystal ball to me and told me to tell everyone what I was seeing.

First of all, this was the first time I had ever seen a crystal ball and second of all, no matter how long and how hard I looked, I didn't see anything, It just looked like a clear crystal ball. Now I knew what that woman had been trying to warn me about Sabrina, It still didn't make sense to me. Sabrina had been doing consulting work for many years and had a very large clientele while I had just started doing consultations and had no following, But I have a habit. When someone challenges me, I try my best to rise to the occasion so I took the crystal ball and pretended I was seeing all sorts of things. Sabrina couldn't challenge me because she had told us different things and she had no way of proving that I hadn't seen a thing and was just making everything up as I went along. She and her friends left shortly after that.

But that was warning enough. The next week Sabrina invited me to a gathering at someone else's house. She said it was to introduce me to her friends. At this point, I was so lonely that I accepted her invitation. We were all sitting around the table when the hostess took out a large, ornate mirror and told us it had magical powers. Supposedly, as you looked into it, you could see yourself in a past life.

One of the women said she saw herself as a Chinese man in a past life. Another woman saw herself as a woman in a large family; she, herself, was an only child in this life. And on and on this went until it came to me. I looked long and hard into this supposedly magic mirror and just saw myself in this current life. I couldn't make up a story because my instincts were telling me that Sabrina had plotted a way to expose me to all her friends. When everyone was gathered around me waiting for me to tell them what I looked like in a past life, I thought, "Well, here goes nothing." So, I \walked away from the mirror and announced to everyone in the room, "I guess it didn't work for me because when I looked in the mirror, I only saw myself as I am now, in these clothes, in this room, in this year." We left shortly after that.

Since I was so new to the group, there was no way for me to judge whether the women were telling the truth or not. One night, I was invited to join the group. Everyone was sitting on the floor in a circle holding up various pieces of jewelry. As I discovered, each of us was to pick up the object that was just handed to them and tell the group something about the previous owner of that piece of jewelry. Once again, I felt as if I was under a microscope being examined for something I couldn't even guess at. Each time an object came to me, I made up something that no one else had said, Once again, it would have been hard to prove because no one else had said it.

Each time I joined this group I felt uncomfortable. I

wasn't being accepted for who I am; they seemed to be waiting for me to make a mistake. To this day, I don't know what, if anything, I did to make them behave that way. In time, they all disappeared, no one saying good-bye to me and I never saw any of them again. I have no idea why they came into my life or what lessons I was supposed to learn from that experience. The only thing I got out of those encounters was that I had to keep my defenses up because I couldn't trust any of them. Maybe that was the lesson I was supposed to learn because until then my attitude was that I should trust everyone until they did something to change my opinion of them. Although I am not as naïve as I used to be, I still tend to be more optimistic and prefer to think well of my fellow man until proven otherwise but now I look more closely at their actions because I have learned that actions speak louder than words.

I find that people don't pay too much attention to their dreams but they pay a little more attention to their visions. Dreams can tell you so much if you know how to interpret them. Some of them are beyond me. I remember reading about a man's dream that told him he was having kidney problems. I lost count as to how many times I read that dream and through the years my memory would hark back to it. I think if it had mentioned plumbing problems, I might have eventually thought of his kidneys but there was no mention of plumbing or water or anything I could associate with it. The same has happened with a few of my dreams that have remained with me through the years, especially one scary one.

When I try to interpret a dream, I first go to the events of the day that just passed, then I look to see a pattern of events that are similar in any way over the days, weeks, or months. Eventually, I can see the connection. When I dream in color it has more of an impact and I tend to remember them longer because I know that it is trying to tell me something of significance.

When my brother was about two years old, he kept waking up at night, crying that a horse had bitten him. We lived in a metropolitan area and I can't remember seeing a single horse yet his nightmares about being bitten by a horse continued for several years. If this had occurred a lifetime later when I had gotten into metaphysics, past lives, and karma, I would have immediately understood that he was reliving a past life traumatic event. Instead, we waited it out because none of us had heard of such things. I even bought a couple of dream books but they were useless. On the other hand, they might have made good movies even though they were clueless about dreams. Since your dreams are about you, very few people can interpret them for you. I often tell people to keep a notebook and a pen or pencil by their bed so they can just reach out and record them. I tried that method for myself but it doesn't work for me, If I'm awakened from a deep sleep it's usually to empty my bladder and by the time I get back to bed, I've forgotten the dream. I always remember when I spend the night dreaming nonstop but I don't remember those dreams. The ones that make the most impact are the ones in color or the ones where I hear voices. I used to hear voices more frequently but now that I'm into metaphysics, I only hear them occasionally; I guess it's to get my attention when all the other methods fail. Nonetheless, I think dreams are very important and when you can interpret them accurately, they can guide you in a way that talking about them cannot.

Visions have always been special for me. I had my first vision when I was seven years old and that vision has not only stayed with me my whole life but it continues to remind me why certain things keep happening in my life that are not meant to change.

When I do my counseling, I pay particular attention

when my clients tell me they had a vision. First of all, I get goosebumps. Second of all, I know they are on a special mission even if neither they nor I don't know what that mission is. But there isn't a doubt in my mind that they are here to serve mankind. I don't know how to describe the difference between a dream and a vision but there is a vast difference. For me, my visions have always appeared during the day, either by themselves or as part of my meditation. Since this is not a topic I usually discuss, I can't give a reliable opinion about how to describe the difference between their appearance, their sound, or their feeling, nor have I ever come across an explanation in a book that mirrors my own experiences with them.

Images are another thing I pay attention to because they act as trigger points to deeply buried memories. Most people overlook them because they don't seem important but, in actuality, they are very important and highly significant. They often act as the key to understanding the root of your problems and that leads you to solve them. Don't make the mistake of thinking that just by understanding the root of your problems they will disappear. They won't. This is just the beginning of your hard work to resolve them and get a new start in a happier life.

There are so many facets to metaphysics and as many books on the subject that I've read or people I've talked to who were supposed to be experts, I've yet to come across anyone who knew more than the basics of it. I don't suppose that we are meant to discover the secrets of the universe, so as curious as I am about piercing the veil between the two worlds, I know this is another one of those infinite secrets that only God is privy to. I just wonder if there will ever come a time when these mysteries will ever be fully unveiled. For now, I must content myself with knowing that as long as it's in God's hands, all's right with the world.

CHAPTER 58

THE AGE OF ENLIGHTENMENT

I remember a time when parents were very concerned about their child's spiritual development. They took their children to Sunday school and they drummed into their heads right from wrong. They taught them that every action has a consequence and they are accountable for everything they do. So where did this concept of spirituality go? Why do we now have so many people with entitlement issues? What are we doing wrong?

Many years ago, when I first became aware that our values were changing, I saw the makings of the new attitude of entitlement in the young and the old. It's the old story of monkey sees, monkey does. I look to the parents to see the example they are setting and I'm astonished at the collapse of our former role models.

In my generation, a parent's word was law. No meant no; it didn't mean maybe and it certainly didn't mean that if I ask you the same thing tomorrow, you'll change your mind and let me have my way. We all knew that there were boundaries and we didn't dare cross them. So what has changed?

Part 'of the changes may be coming from the shift in the role models we now have. Women were considered the heart of the home. They cooked and cleaned and supervised their child's homework. In short, they were the unpaid laborers whose work went unappreciated. It was also their duty to teach their children a spiritual code of ethics, another part of their job that went unappreciated and unrecognized.

It's no wonder that we had a feminist movement comprised of women who were tired of being seen as second-class citizens, of very little value. The problem with that was that they threw the baby out with the bathwater. Now, not only were they not seen as equal to men, but their children began rebelling against their authority.

About the time that these changes were taking place, I was in a supermarket and I heard a woman trying to get her child to stop screaming. I walked over to them and asked what was wrong. The woman looked frazzled. She told me that her child wanted her to buy him candy but she only had enough money to buy some inexpensive food for dinner. I saw that he was small enough to sit in the top part of the shopping cart but he had powerful lungs that could shatter glass.

"Ignore him. Let him scream his lungs out. He'll knock himself out and stop screaming," I said. She looked at me and shook her head. "He'll disturb the other shoppers," she replied. I tried a different tactic. "How old is he?" I asked. "He just turned three, "she replied. "And you're letting a three-year-old pull your strings and manipulate you? I can't wait to see the damage he causes by the time he turns five," I told her. About an hour later, our paths crossed again. This time the toddler had chocolate smeared all over his face, wearing a very satisfied expression and there were no groceries in the mother's cart.

I thought about that little boy and his mother all the way home. Is this the new way of raising children these days? I pondered. No wonder we're breeding a new wave of entitled children who will grow up into obnoxious entitled adults.

Several months later, a woman brought her five-year-old boy into our pediatric office. I tried to get him on the scale to weigh and measure him but he wouldn't budge. His mother said nothing and did nothing. Then, the little boy kicked me very hard in the shin, and still, his mother said and did nothing. No help there so I kicked the boy in his shin. And still no comment from his mother; she just stood there watching us. Then, the boy lifted his hand and made a fist so I lifted my hand and made a fist. He took one look at my eyes which were filled with determination and he lowered his fist and climbed on the scale. After that, he was good as gold whenever he came into our office.

During the years that I worked in pediatrics, I witnessed countless children manipulating their mothers and these women acted as though they were the victims. These little terrors had more tricks up their sleeves and their parents just shrugged their shoulders as if their children were running the show.

But a ten-year-old child taught me the most about the lengths a child will go to get his way. A mother brought her son in for a camp examination and he was throwing a tantrum. "If you send me to camp, I'll have an asthma attack and they'll have to send me home." His mother didn't say a word. A few weeks later, he joined the other boys on the camp bus and that night he had a severe asthma attack and his father was called to take him home.

It was clear that he knew how to bring on an asthma attack and he used it every time he wanted to get his way. Now he was free to spend the summer with his friends and his parents were powerless to stop him. In keeping with teaching him spiritual values, I would have told him that if he didn't go to camp, he would be confined to the house all summer. No cell phone, no television, no friends, no nothing. I would also have told him that he would be doing chores around the house all summer. He wouldn't even be allowed to read a book because books should never be used as punishment.

At the end of that summer, this boy was riding high. No expectations were made of him. He was able to play with his friends, watch television, use his cell phone, and not do a single chore around the house. I can't imagine him growing up and being a useful member of society, and I certainly can't imagine him living his life dedicated to being of service to humanity.

What I can imagine is him sponging off his friends and getting away with as much as he can with as little effort as he has to make to survive.

I know that his parents go to their house of worship and he goes to Sunday school. They probably count that as being spiritual. My take on that is spiritual is as spiritual does and giving donations instead of service doesn't count as spiritual.

The big task for humanity is to figure out how to be happy with what you have and how to experience the joy of giving and sharing. The bigger task will be to teach people how to be grateful for everything they have and to rid themselves of the attitude of entitlement. No one is entitled to anything. Even the air we breathe is a blessing, not an entitlement. But most of all, our biggest blessing is having the ability to make a difference in someone's life without the expectation of receiving something in return. That's spirituality at its highest peak.

CHAPTER 59

SUPERMAN'S KRYPTONITE

Fear is one of the most paralyzing emotions we can ever experience. It stops us from living life to the fullest and cripples our need for freedom and independence. Imagine yourself dreaming of going on a kayak with your friends and because you are so afraid of drowning, you decline the invitation. You don't know anyone who drowned but you have refused to take swimming lessons. You've missed out on parties that were too near the lake even though you could have stayed at the shallow end of the lake but even that was too daunting for you to try.

What are your options? You live near the water and you

have a group of very nice friends. If you keep declining their invitations, they will eventually stop asking you to join them. Are you prepared to live like a recluse, because if you aren't, then you need to take some drastic steps to overcome this irrational fear. I call it irrational because you have no reason to be afraid of drowning if you never knew anyone who had a swimming accident or drowned.

Sometimes we build things up in our mind and we don't know why we did but we can't seem to undo it. It doesn't take long for these things to escalate into fears that become too difficult to change. This is where good counseling can help get to the root of the problem and solve it fairly quickly since it hasn't impeded your daily life over too many years.

One of my clients was the living proof of that. When she came for her appointment, the first thing she said to me was "I need help in changing something that is ruining my life." She was a very successful attorney...up to a point. It seems as though she found it impossible to go up against any male attorney. She prepared her cases very thoroughly but when it came time to present her arguments, she would take a look at the male attorney who was opposing her and go into freeze mode.

There was no logical reason for her to feel intimidated

by male attorneys. She was pretty, dressed professionally, was very smart, and always prepared her cases meticulously. She won most of her cases that were represented by female attorneys but couldn't win a case against male attorneys. I told her I could help her but it would require her doing some offbeat homework assignments. She agreed and we proceeded.

I told her that she would have to buy or rent a Superman costume, complete with the red boots, the blue bodysuit with the red "S" on the inverted triangle on the chest, the red pants that look like men's briefs, the yellow belt, and the red cape. Her assignment was to put on this Superman costume every day and stand on a bed. When she was in the costume and standing on the bed, she was to let herself feel powerful and, then she had to say the famous words: "Faster than a speeding bullet... More powerful than a locomotive...Able to leap tall buildings in a single bound. Look! Up in the sky...It's a bird... It's a plane . . . It's Superman." Then, she was to jump off the bed as if she was flying.

I had her vary the monologue so she would have to think about what she was saying. If you keep saying the same words over and over, it's not only monotonous but it loses the impact of the message to the brain. In her case, the message to the brain was the reason I gave her this homework assignment and it proved to be very successful.

A few months after she started the assignment there was a tremendous change in her. She started looking men in the eyes and taking on opposing male attorneys in court. Now, instead of the men thinking when they saw her in court that they were going to have an easy win, they got the shock of their lives. She won case after case against some of the most experienced attorneys and became a force to be reckoned with.

About a year later, she came to me for another distressing problem and I assured her that we could resolve the problem but that it would require a weird homework assignment. She looked at me and asked, "The Superman costume wasn't weird?"

CHAPTER 60

IN MY OPINION . . .

I have long held the belief that all clergymen, of all religions, male or female, should hold outside jobs and not be supported by their congregation.

People are always saying that clergymen spend a lot of time going to hospitals and praying over, or with, the sick and the dying. They spend a lot of time writing their weekly sermons, counseling their congregants, and studying. All of which may or may not be true but it still isn't reason enough to be supported by their congregation.

I remember a group of us met every week in a place that was very run-down and barely affordable. We eventually decided that we should hire a clergyman and make it official. We took up funds to hire one and, although most of us were struggling to pay our own mortgage, we bought a house for our clergyman and paid the monthly mortgage on his house.

We had volunteers mowing his lawn, cleaning his house, cooking for him, and doing his laundry. It wasn't that he wasn't appreciative; it was more like he expected us to do those things for him.

During those years, I noticed that our clergyman played tennis every morning and other clergymen played golf several times a week. They had a lot of spare time that the rest of us did not have.

At the time, I was working sixty hours a week and going to school at night, in addition to having my own household to run. And still, I was one of the congregants who shared some of the jobs for our clergyman.

We were the ones who made the telephone calls to let members know of upcoming events and to round up volunteers to man booths for cake sales, sell raffle tickets, get store owners to contribute items for our bazaars, etc. And all this time, our clergyman found time to get out on the tennis court each morning.

It was during those years of observing various clergymen from all the different religions who were supported by their congregations, who were doing much less work than we were and who had a lot of time for recreation, that led me down the path of critical thinking about the clergy.

My conclusions were that most of us visited hospitals to comfort the sick and the dying and we weren't paid to do it. Clergymen accept donations for saying prayers and delivering eulogies at funerals. They call it donations but it's really an expected fee.

But I once knew a woman who was a professional mourner although she did it without collecting a cent. Every day she would read the obituaries in the newspaper and go to whatever funerals were scheduled that day. She would sit in the pew (any religion) and cry and wail as though she were a grieving relative.

I never had the nerve to ask her if she was crying for the deceased or if she was crying for herself but it obviously filled some part of her emotional self to go to these funerals and mourn for the ones being buried.

Most of us try to help people who have problems. We counsel them, listen to their troubles, and give them hope for a better tomorrow. And most of us have had relationship experiences to draw from when people come to us with their problems. The same can't be said about many clergymen who counsel their congregants about their marriage difficulties without ever having been married or without having to experience their own intimacy issues.

Many of us have spent some of our lives studying, even though we have had households to run and full-time jobs to go to in the morning. And this is just a part of life. There is always the thought, there, but for the grace of God, go I, and so we heed the call of human misery and do what we can to help when the need arises.

Yes, a clergyman has studied more about religion than the rest of us but he is no more spiritual than the rest of us and he has no more understanding of the nature of God than the rest of us. He isn't a direct link to God, although many clergymen would have us believe otherwise.

We may even have studied comparative religions and metaphysics. Perhaps not as much as a clergyman but more than enough to see that clergymen have feet of clay like the rest of us. They err. They do noble things. They do immoral or illegal things. They are human and they behave as humans; no more, no less.

We have seen the sharp decline of religion. We have also seen the sharp decline of spirituality. And, no, religiosity is not the same thing as spirituality. You can be very religious and not be the least bit spiritual and you can be very spiritual and not believe in organized religion.

There is no one path to anything; there are infinite paths to everything. Somehow, I don't think that financially supporting clergymen is the way to bring people closer to God. When I think about the myriad paths to accomplish this, I think about a path that involves a whole congregation or a whole community where everyone has a stake in the way they seek God.

Instead of a clergyman writing weekly sermons, let everyone in the congregation take a turn at delivering a sermon. They can talk about their own experiences or talk about things that are going on in the world. They can talk about faith, hope, and love. They can talk about service to mankind, charity, and prejudice. And they can tie all of these topics back to God and what it means to them to feel a connection to God.

People have always made time in their lives to visit sick people in hospitals, to take care of the elderly, the impoverished, the needy. Whenever someone is truly sick or had to bury a loved one, they are often surprised at the number of people who bring casseroles to feed their families for however long it's needed.

When clergymen are allowed to be seen as human, and not as mini-gods, they can contribute to this community of caring while being gainfully employed elsewhere. And it's this community of caring that is the bedrock of spirituality and every religion in the world.

If people are allowed to contribute the essence of their being to a common cause, rather than their money, we will see a return to God that has the power to unite all mankind, bound by love and forgiveness, and the knowledge that there is no such thing as only one path to enlightenment and anyone who truly desires it can achieve it.

God would not have made so many races and so many cultural differences if He thought that everyone should walk the same path and have the same beliefs. I think there must be an infinite number of paths and each of us is destined to walk one of those paths that will eventually bring us back to God.

ABOUT THE AUTHOR

Connie H. Deutsch is an author, renowned consultant and spiritual advisor who has a keen understanding of human nature and is a natural problem-solver. She is known throughout the world for helping clients find workable solutions to problems that are often complex and systemic in nature and part of a corporation's culture or an individual's pattern of behavior.

Connie's depth of experience lends itself to both corporate consulting and individual counseling. Perhaps Connie is best known for her "homework" assignments which serve as virtual road maps for moving clients through problems into living solutions.

In addition to her consulting and counseling practice, Connie has hosted her own weekly radio show, is a regular contributor to the spiritual and personal growth website *Next Level Soul* (www.nextlevelsoul.com) and is one of the most downloaded guests ever on the popular *Next Level Soul with Alex Ferrari* podcast.

She has been a guest on numerous cable, radio shows, and podcasts around the country. She wrote a weekly advice column for sixteen years and has been has been invited to speak at universities around the world.

Visit her website at www.ConnieHDeutsch.com

next level SOUL™

<u>*Next Level Soul*</u>™ is a resource for spiritual seekers, and curious souls who are looking to find the deeper meaning in their lives. On NLS you will learn from some of the world's top spiritual and thought leaders. To help you on your spiritual path NLS publishes books, audiobooks, courses, weekly podcasts, and videos. We are here to help you on your life's journey and awaken your inner peace.

Next Level Soul™ founder, Alex Ferrari is a #1 best-selling author, speaker, entrepreneur, award-winning filmmaker, spiritual seeker and podcaster. His industry leading podcasts, the Webby award-nominated Indie Film Hustle, and Bulletproof Screenwriting have been downloaded over 11 million times to date. He has had the pleasure of speaking to icons like Oscar®

Winner *Oliver Stone* and *Billy Crystal,* music legends like *Bruce Dickinson* (Iron Maiden) and *Moby* (Grammy® Award Winning Music Icon), actors like *Edward Burns* (Saving Private Ryan) and *Eva Longoria* (Desperate Housewives), thought leaders like 2X Nobel Prize Nominee *Dr. Ervin Laszlo* and *Dr. Eben Alexander* (Proof of Heaven) and New York Times Best-Selling authors Dan Millman (The Way of the Peaceful Warrior) and Dr. Raymond Moody (Life After Life).

Throughout his life's journey Alex was always asking the big questions. Why are we here? Is this all there is? What is my soul's mission in this life? He developed NLS to help people around the world get closer to their own higher power; to look inward for the answers they are searching for.

The *Next Level Soul™ Podcast* was created to help answer those questions by having raw and inspiring conversations with some of the most fascinating and thought provoking souls on the planet today.

For more information on Next Level Soul:

Official Site: www.nextlevelsoul.com
Next Level Soul Podcast: www.nextlevelsoul.com/podcast
Next Level Soul Books: www.nextlevelsoul.com/books

THOUGHTS AND REFLECTIONS

I wanted to create a space for you to write down your thoughts and reflections after reading sections of the book. Think of this as your own personal addition to the book. Look inside yourself and write down what you are feeling right now. You will thank yourself in the future.

236 • A SOUL'S GUIDE TO METAPHYSICS AND SPIRITUALITY

CONNIE H. DEUTSCH • 237

238 • A SOUL'S GUIDE TO METAPHYSICS AND SPIRITUALITY

CONNIE H. DEUTSCH • 239

240 • A SOUL'S GUIDE TO METAPHYSICS AND SPIRITUALITY

CONNIE H. DEUTSCH • 241

242 • A SOUL'S GUIDE TO METAPHYSICS AND SPIRITUALITY

CONNIE H. DEUTSCH • 243

244 • A SOUL'S GUIDE TO METAPHYSICS AND SPIRITUALITY

Printed in Great Britain
by Amazon

Cricket and National Identity in the Postcolonial Age

Mention cricket, and some still think of the gentle game played on a village green in England, where leather thuds against willow, slumbering spectators mutter 'Good shot, sir' and church bells toll in the middle distance . . . But this cricket – and that England – is as outdated as the idea of Empire, and the game today is as much about cable television, huge crowds at one-day internationals in Mumbai or Islamabad, or floodlit Twenty20 games timed to maximise broadcast advertising revenue.

Bringing together leading writers on cricket and society, this important new book places cricket in the postcolonial life of the major Test-playing countries, exploring the culture, politics, governance and economics of cricket in the twenty-first century. It covers

- Cricket in the new Commonwealth: in Sri Lanka, Pakistan, the Caribbean and India
- The cricket cultures of Australia, New Zealand and post-apartheid South Africa
- Cricket in England since the 1950s

Cricket and National Identity in the Postcolonial Age is an original political and historical study of the game's development in a range of countries. Ideal for students of sport, politics, history and postcolonialism, it provides accessible and stimulating discussion of the major issues, including race, migration, globalisation, neoliberal economics, religion and sectarianism and the media.

Stephen Wagg is Reader in Sport and Society at Roehampton University, UK. He has written widely on the politics of sport, of the media, of comedy and of childhood.